BRITAIN'S TREES

... *move along these shades*
In gentleness of heart; with gentle hand
Touch — for there is a spirit in the woods.

WILLIAM WORDSWORTH, FROM
'NUTTING' (1798–9)

BRITAIN'S TREES

JO WOOLF

National Trust

To Ann and Eric

First published in the United Kingdom in 2020 by
National Trust Books
43 Great Ormond Street
London
WC1N 3HZ

An imprint of Pavilion Books Company Ltd

ISBN 978-1-91135-886-2

A CIP catalogue record for this book is available from the British Library.

10 9 8 7 6 5 4 3 2 1

Reproduction by Rival Colour Ltd, UK
Printed and bound by 1010 Printing International Ltd, China

This book can be ordered direct from the publisher
at www.pavilionbooks.com

Interior illustrations by Louise Morgan

CONTENTS

INTRODUCTION

One impulse from a vernal wood
May teach you more of man
Of moral evil and of good
Than all the sages can.

WILLIAM WORDSWORTH, FROM 'THE TABLES TURNED',
LYRICAL BALLADS (1798)

One of the lovely things about trees is that, just by standing beneath them and gazing up into their branches, we can feel a sense of reassurance and calm. We may also feel an empathy, however faint, with generations of people stretching back into our most distant past. Trees, after all, were part of our landscape long before we even set foot here; it feels as if they are woven into our genetic make-up, half-forgotten but ever-present, a reminder, if we will take the time to hear it, of the natural cycle of life and death, of decay and rebirth. Compared to us, in our daily rush across the surface of the Earth, trees are static: it is easy to forget that they are living beings at all. But they can teach us so much. Their 'pulse' may be slower, their wavelength longer ... yet their wisdom is deep, and their gift is infinite.

At the end of the last glacial period, estimated to be around 12,500 years ago, the freshly exposed landscape that we now know as Britain began to rise up once again after millennia of being crushed by ice; and into this fertile terrain came the seeds of pioneering trees: birch, aspen and sallow, followed by pine, hazel, alder, oak, lime and elm. By about 4500BC, the prehistoric 'wildwoods' of Britain were at their peak; small groups of early humans would have travelled the land in pursuit of elk, red and roe deer and aurochs, gathering nuts and berries and living in seasonal shelters.

Our earliest understanding of trees would have been instinctive, based on recognising the properties of different species; over time, and with contributions from a multitude of different cultures, this understanding was interpreted into tradition and folklore, and as remedies for all kinds of ailments, however strange or outrageous they might appear to us today. Such wisdom was passed on simply by word of mouth; it is only in comparatively recent times that we have started to record our ideas, history and stories. Writing, quite often, demands logical explanations when there are none: listeners sitting around an Iron Age fire would have found little to question, and may well have added embellishments of their own at the next retelling. For them, there were no boundaries between history, lore and legend.

Britain's rich blend of cultures is evident in our interpretation of trees, and certainly in the way we use them. When we walk in the woods, we can almost hear the sage voices of druids, the battle cries of Norse warriors, the proclamations of Anglo-Saxon kings. With this in mind, it is fascinating to learn more about our trees: which species, for example, were fashioned into shields and why? Which twigs were carried as talismans, and which trees were to be avoided when setting out on a journey? Were elder trees growing around your house regarded as a good or a bad thing? And why should you never dig up a hawthorn? These are old stories whose origins are lost, but don't be fooled into thinking they are obsolete: many of our tree-related superstitions are still practised, quietly and carefully, perhaps even unconsciously. The last time you expressed hope for a good outcome did you use the phrase 'touch wood'?

In the eyes of our ancestors, trees were the home of ethereal beings – elves and dryads, gods and goddesses, witches and fairies, who could be mischievous, benevolent or vengeful according to their whim. Some trees were seen as a portal to the underworld, while others transmitted spirit messages through their leaves. While most of our surviving ancient monuments are made of stone, it is interesting to ponder how many wooden structures may have been lost. At Woodhenge in Wiltshire, concentric rings of post holes are the ghosts of a large building whose purpose we can only conjecture; and at Seahenge on Holme Beach in Norfolk, wooden posts encircle the trunk of a huge oak tree that was deliberately positioned upside down – the relic, perhaps, of some ceremony that took place in the early Bronze Age.

A regular glimpse into our medieval past is offered in the form of village festivals, many of which involve trees in some shape or form. Through centuries-old songs and processions, the fears and hopes of former generations come alive again before our eyes: the midwinter 'wassailing' of orchards, the May Day processions and maypole dancing, the kindling of Samhain fires at Halloween. Figures such as the Green Man or Jack in the Green symbolise rebirth and renewal, while morris dancers wield their rods of hazel and the Nitch Ladies of Great Wishford carry their sprigs of oak into Salisbury Cathedral. Birch branches are still used in many places in 'beating the bounds', a ceremony that reaffirmed the boundaries of a parish to all its inhabitants.

Looking at the countless remedies and potions that have been handed down to us over the centuries, it seems that there is no ailment for which a tree cannot offer some kind of cure. For wounds and burns, leaves were made into a soothing poultice, and the shoots of some trees were chewed to relieve pain long before modern research identified the anti-inflammatory and antiseptic compounds that they contain. Restorative infusions were made from bark and roots, certain berries would ease a sore throat, and if none of that worked there was a battery of superstitions to fall back on, some of them simply demanding that the sufferer carry a twig or a nut in his pocket, and others necessitating a degree of discipline, faith or magic, depending on the patient's point of view.

Under certain circumstances, individual trees were believed to be capable of miraculous healing: weary pilgrims would tie scraps of cloth to trees that grew by sacred wells, and the strange power of a 'shrew-ash' even exerted itself over stiff-backed Victorians. Trees had a darker role, too: the corpses of criminals would be left dangling from the long limbs of hanging-trees as a stark warning to would-be offenders. Convicted witches, after execution, were often buried with a stake through the heart just for good measure; the knowledge of which tree to carve it from was crucial to the question of whether he or she would rise again and cause further trouble.

In medieval Ireland, it seems that the knowledge of trees was less of a science and more of an art form. In an ancient poem known as *Aidedh Ferghusa meic Léide,* the king of the fairies holds forth on the individual properties of trees as firewood, while the ruler of Ulster and all his courtiers listen. They are told that the trees themselves are imbued with magical properties, such as the elder that furnishes armies with horses from the fairy realm, and the ash that turns battle into flight. Some, like the willow, should not be burned, as it is a tree 'sacred to poems', while the holly and the oak are the best providers of heat. Meanwhile in the *Book of Taliesin,* one of the four ancient books of Wales, a poem known as the *Cad Goddeu* describes a battle between the trees themselves: a sorcerer, Gwydion, uses a staff to transform them into warriors, and tribute is paid to each in turn.

Ogham script, an early form of writing that originated in Ireland, is still preserved in some precious examples of stone carvings. Different versions of the Ogham alphabet have been proposed by scholars, but some of the oldest symbols are understood to represent trees – for example, *beith*, meaning 'birch', and *feàrn*, meaning 'alder'. Some historians have speculated that every symbol may have had its own corresponding tree. It is interesting also to consider that the words 'tree' and 'trust' both stem from the Old English *treow*. This may help to explain why an ancient oak or yew, steadfast witness to centuries of history, was often chosen as a venue for important discussions and decision-making.

Throughout the ages, trees have played a significant role in literature. Shakespeare, for example, often compares his characters to trees, or uses them to enhance the atmosphere of a scene; sometimes the story hangs on the behaviour of the trees themselves. The Romantic poets looked to the trees for inspiration and found beauty, joy and sadness. William Wordsworth and Samuel Taylor Coleridge regularly composed poetry in the woods, and John Keats declared that '... if poetry comes not as naturally as the leaves to a tree, it had better not come at all'. Thomas Hardy, in weaving his tales of love and tragedy in rural Wessex, endowed his characters with an intuitive understanding of the English landscape. 'To dwellers in a wood,' he wrote in *Under the Greenwood Tree*, 'every species of tree has its voice as well as its feature.'

The question of which trees to include in this book was one that demanded careful consideration. In addition to our native trees, which arrived with no human assistance, it was important also to include archaeophytes or ancient introductions; I have also included some trees that are comparative newcomers, but now feature prominently in our landscape. This task reminded me that our countryside is constantly changing – sometimes rapidly, and sometimes over centuries so that the shift is almost imperceptible in a human lifetime. Certain species have been repeatedly ravaged by disease, and some are making a defiant comeback. All we can do is lend them all the support we can and take time to fully appreciate the trees that are here now, in our own lifetimes – and teach our children and grandchildren to do the same.

Recent evidence shows that trees are far more responsive and intelligent than we think. For instance, they can identify the saliva of certain insects munching on their leaves and call on small parasitic wasps to come and feed on them. Trees of the same species growing together can communicate via fungal networks around their root tips, as well as by electrical impulses. In some ways, trees are an analogy of what we aspire to be – grounded in our awareness and dependence upon the Earth, interconnected to our own mutual benefit, strong yet pliant in the face of storms, and patient in the knowledge that spring sunshine will always return. Perhaps this is why trees, for more centuries than we can count, have always played such a major role in our survival, in our history, and in our affections. We are more like trees than we realise: no matter how far apart we appear to be, in terms of geographical distance or ancestral origin, we have all arisen from the same root, and we are all individual leaves of the same tree.

NOTES ON THE TEXT

COPPICING AND POLLARDING

Coppicing and pollarding are two terms that I use quite often in this book. Both are traditional methods of pruning, designed to encourage fresh growth in a living tree so that its wood can be harvested repeatedly. While coppicing is done at ground level, pollarding involves removing branches at a height of about 7–8ft (2–2.5m), beyond the reach of grazers. The new shoots are then cut for a multitude of uses such as firewood, fencing or cattle fodder. A coppiced wood is sometimes called a copse, and an individual tree that has been coppiced is known as a stool.

FLOWERS

The flowers of trees are sometimes showy and distinctive, while others can be small and hard to spot. Some trees, such as oaks, bear both male and female flowers separately on the same tree, and are described as monoecious. Others, like holly and yew, carry male and female flowers on different trees, and are described as dioecious. Wild cherry and crab apple are among those trees that are hermaphroditic, meaning that both male and female parts are contained in the same flower.

FAMOUS BOTANISTS

Throughout this book, I refer to some influential works by authors whose legacy is still celebrated after several centuries. They were colourful characters themselves, with strong opinions that influenced monarchs and probably helped to save lives …

John Gerard (*c.* 1545–1612) was an English botanist whose *Herball, or Generall Historie of Plantes* was first published in 1597 and became hugely popular. Gerard referred to the works of early Greek writers as well as his contemporaries, speaking of the 'vertues' or properties of plants. With a reputation as a skilled herbalist, he worked for 20 years as superintendent of the gardens of William Cecil, the famous advisor to Elizabeth I, and was also curator of the Physic Garden at the College of Physicians.

Nicholas Culpeper (1616–1654) was a botanist, a herbalist, a physician and a rebel. He set up a pharmacy in Spitalfields, London, using various fields of science, including astrology, to treat his many patients. His abiding belief was that medicinal knowledge should be shared with the general population, rather than kept as the secret preserve of the Royal College of Physicians. To this end, in 1652 he published a collection of his remedies in an affordable volume called *The English Physitian*, which later became known as Culpeper's Complete Herbal.

John Evelyn (1620–1706) was a philosopher and founding member of the Royal Society who enjoyed close ties to the royal court of Charles II. His great literary triumph, *Sylva, or, A discourse of forest-trees, and the propagation of timber in His Majesties dominions* (1664) was a landmark treatise on the management of trees. The work had begun life as a report, written in response to an appeal by the Royal Navy to address a shortage of timber for shipbuilding. But *Sylva* had a much wider impact, helping to change our perceptions of trees and forests and inspiring generations of landowners to improve the management of their woodlands.

THE WORK OF THE NATIONAL TRUST

Appropriately for a charity whose emblem is an oak sprig with acorns, the National Trust cares for 26,000 hectares (64,000 acres) of woodland throughout England, Wales and Northern Ireland, and is dedicated to conserving and protecting them from the spread of disease. Many diseases affect one species in particular: ash dieback, for instance, was first confirmed in the UK in 2012 and poses a serious threat to our ash population. The disease is caused by a fungus, *Hymenoscyphus fraxineus*, and causes leaf loss and crown dieback. The National Trust is taking all possible steps to help tackle the disease on its land, and is also working with the Forestry Commission, the Woodland Trust, the Food and Environment Research Agency and Defra.

Our oak trees are threatened by pests and diseases such as oak processionary moth and acute oak decline. The National Trust is one of several charities involved in the Action Oak Partnership which is funding research, monitoring changes in the oak population, and working with owners and managers of trees and woodlands. Other species such as box and juniper have recorded instances of specific fungal attack, and the National Trust is working with other organisations such as the Royal Horticultural Society and Plantlife in efforts to find solutions. They deserve our wholehearted support.

A WARNING

There are few tree species that do not have at least one age-old medicinal use. Some of these remedies have since been borne out by science, while others continue to baffle us with their weirdness. Under no circumstances should any of the information contained in this book be interpreted as medical guidance.

ALDER

Alnus glutinosa

Alders have a gentle, almost ethereal presence, which seems to hover between the realms of earth and water. These trees flourish in damp areas, often bending low over tumbling streams and tranquil pools, their roots submerged in the wet ground. They are neither tall nor showy, but in the eyes of our ancestors few trees held more significance in terms of protection and prophecy.

The bright green, almost pear-shaped leaves are quite distinctive, being deeply veined and slightly indented at the tip. Dark pink female flowers appear in early spring, before the leaves are out; more conspicuous are the male catkins, golden lambs' tails that are slightly more compact than those of hazel. After pollination, cone-shaped green fruits ripen and release reddish-brown seeds; if these drop into water they can survive for at least a year, thanks to little pockets of air that give them a natural buoyancy. Fast-flowing rivers carry them away to colonise new areas downstream, and meanwhile the dry, empty cones remain on the tree until the following spring.

As a food plant, the tree is host to several moths including the delightfully named alder kitten; alder catkins are an early source of nectar and pollen for bees, and the seeds are eaten by birds such as siskins and redpolls. Alder has an important symbiotic relationship with a bacterium, *Frankia alni*, which forms nodules on its roots. These absorb nitrogen from the air and make it available to the tree; in return, the alder provides the bacteria with carbon. In this way, alder improves the fertility of the soil where it grows, creating nutrients for species that follow it onto new ground.

The value of alder was not always recognised by landowners, much to the disgust of John Evelyn in the seventeenth century: 'There are a sort of husbands,' he wrote, 'who take excessive pains in stubbing up their alders, where-ever they meet them in the boggie places of their grounds, with the same indignation as one would extirpate the most pernicious of weeds; and when they have finished, know not how to convert their best lands to more profit than this (seeming despicable) plant might lead them to, were it rightly understood.' (*Sylva*)

Alder's strength lies in its resistance to decay, even under water. The cities of Venice and Amsterdam were built upon alder piles: once submerged, the wood gradually becomes as hard as stone. For this reason, Neolithic settlers chose it for building tracks over the Somerset Levels, while in Scotland, Iron Age island dwellings known as crannogs were constructed on beds made of alder trunks. When exposed to the air, however, waterlogged alder quickly begins to decompose.

In England, alder woods were often called 'carrs' from the Old Norse *kjarr*, meaning a swamp, and the 'carr' element has been preserved in some place names. In addition, places such as Allerton, Allerbeck and Ellerslie recall the existence of an alder wood. The old Gaelic word for alder is *feàrn*: author Gavin Maxwell's house on Skye was called Camusfeàrna, 'the bay of alders'. The Welsh form is *gwern*, sometimes mutated to *wern*, and these crop up so often in the east of Wales that historians have wondered whether alder trees were grown there commercially in medieval times, so that their timber could be sold to rich Norman estates in Herefordshire and Shropshire. The theory is that the wood may have been made into clogs for farm workers.

> *In the Welsh Mabinogion, the alder is the emblem of the Celtic giant-god, Brân*

In the Welsh *Mabinogion*, the alder is the emblem of the Celtic giant-god, Brân. One story tells how Brân's sister, Branwen, was being mistreated by her husband, Matholwch, King of Ireland. Brân calls his men together and sets off to rescue her; when they come to the River Llinon, they find that the only bridge has been dismantled on the orders of the Irish king, so Brân lies down across the river to allow the men to pass over his body. This may be a reference to the alder's natural empathy with water.

Sure-hoofed is my steed impelled by the spur;
The high springs of alder on thy shield;
Brân thou art called, of the glittering branches.

Sure-hoofed is my steed in the day of battle:
The high sprigs of alder are in thy hand:
Brân thou art, by the branch thou bearest
Has Amaethon the Good prevailed!

TRANSLATION OF WELSH *ENGLYN* ASSOCIATED WITH THE *CAD GODDEU*, 'THE BATTLE OF THE TREES' IN THE FOURTEENTH-CENTURY *BOOK OF TALIESIN*

Once it has been cut down, the pale wood of alder turns deep orange and releases a reddish sap; it can almost appear as if the tree is bleeding. Perhaps it was this phenomenon that earned alder its reputation as the 'tree of war', inspiring early warriors to carve it into shields. One example is the Kiltubbrid Shield, an Iron Age relic

ALDER
Catkins and cones

which was unearthed from a bog in County Leitrim, Ireland, in the nineteenth century.

In spite of their love for the qualities of its wood, the Irish considered it unlucky to pass an alder tree on a journey. This may derive from the fact that alder groves were usually dark, boggy places where evil spirits were thought to dwell. Given the widespread distribution of alder, this must have given rise to some lengthy journeys! It was also believed that putting some alder leaves in your shoes at the start of a long walk would cool the feet and prevent soreness.

Is there any more romantic name than Deirdre of the Sorrows? According to an Irish legend, the royal storyteller at the court of King Conchobar mac Nessa had a beautiful daughter named Deirdre. She was destined to marry the king, but she fell in love with Naoise, a handsome warrior. To escape the king's wrath, Deirdre and Naoise fled across the sea to Scotland where they hid in the alder woods of Glen Etive. They were tracked down by Conchobar's men who murdered Naoise and brought Deirdre back to Ulster where she was forced into marriage. One version of the story says that she took her own life by throwing herself from a chariot.

Just as enigmatic as Deirdre, but slightly more tangible, is the Ballachulish Goddess. In 1880 a small female figure, carved from a single piece of alder with pebbles for eyes, was recovered from a peat bog on the shore of Loch Leven near Ballachulish. It is thought to date from somewhere between 728 and 524BC.

Brown, red and green fabric dyes were made from the twigs, bark and flowers, and it was said that fairies' clothes were also dyed with alder to conceal them from human eyes. Both the bark and the wood contain tannin, a substance used for tanning leather. Fresh alder leaves are said to make a good insect repellent, and dried leaves were placed in a bed or a cushion to relieve rheumatism. With antibacterial properties, a decoction of alder bark was applied to wounds and inflammations. The wood burns with an intense heat, making it an ideal fire for forging weapons, and Bronze Age archaeological finds have revealed the use of alder to make charcoal.

To our forebears, alder was the tree of prophecy and sacrifice: smoke from alder fires was used for divination, as was the movement of the flames. On the living tree, omens were seen in the way the branches moved, and in the rustle of the leaves. Whistles made from alder wood were said to summon the wind and enlist the help of benevolent water spirits. More recently, the guitar manufacturer Fender uses alder to build the bodies of its electric guitars, including the famous Stratocaster, as it delivers clarity and a full-bodied tone.

> *Alder tree! O alder tree!*
> *Is it a voice of sorrow*
> *That sighs 'mong thy leaves in the silent night,*
> *When the radiant hue of the moonshine bright*
> *Announceth a pleasant morrow?*
>
> CHARLES MACKAY, FROM 'THE ALDER TREE', *SONGS AND POEMS* (1834)

CRAB APPLE

Malus sylvestris

Native to Britain and Ireland, the crab apple or 'wilding' can often be found growing in old hedges and on the fringes of woodland. In autumn, a shower of yellowish-green fruits litters the ground beneath: these are small, hard and extremely acid. In spring, the branches are decked with a profusion of white blossom, opening from demure pink buds; a wild apple tree in bloom is a joy to behold.

This fey hedgerow beauty was an earlier arrival than the first domestic apples, which were transported across Asia on the Silk Road. Crab apple can be distinguished from garden escapees by its hairless flower stalks and undersurfaces of the leaves. It is widespread but uncommon and is sometimes regarded as an indicator of ancient woodland. Over the centuries, the crab apple may have had little to do with the cultivation of its orchard-grown cousins, but its fruits still found many culinary uses.

Crab apple jelly is made by stewing the whole fruits, passing the cooked pulp through a fine sieve, and then boiling it with sugar. The fermented juice was turned into cider and wine, and the pantries of medieval cooks would include a liquid called 'verjuice' or 'vargis', a bitter brew, also made from fermented juice, which was used in the same way that we might use lemon juice. In a tart of domestic apples, a couple of 'crabs' enhanced the flavour.

> *In spring, the branches are decked with a profusion of white blossom, opening from demure pink buds*

Some historians believe that the word 'crab' in this context comes from the Old English, *crabbe*, meaning 'of bitter or sharp taste'. In *Wayside and Woodland Trees* (1904), however, Edward Step considers that it may derive from the Anglo-Saxon *scrobb*, meaning 'a shrub'.

Until the seventeenth century, the word 'apple' was widely used to describe any fruit, meaning that the forbidden fruit eaten by Adam and Eve could easily have been a fig or a quince, for example; it is

21

CRAB APPLE
Fruit

interesting to note, however, that *Malus*, the Latin word for apple, means 'evil' when used as an adjective.

Apple wood is extremely hard and tough and was once used to build the working parts of corn mills, as well as for fine furniture, drawing instruments, and engraving. It makes a fragrant firewood and burns to produce good-quality charcoal: in the woods of the Lake District, apple trees can be found growing next to old charcoal-burning sites. A yellow dye, once used for wool, was extracted from the bark.

> *The juyce of wilde Apples or crabs taketh away the heat of burnings, scaldings, and all inflammations; and being laid on in short time after it is scalded, it keepeth it from blistering.*
> JOHN GERARD, FROM *THE HERBALL* (1597)

Apple juice was also recommended by Gerard to ease a horrible affliction known as St Anthony's fire, caused by poisoning from a fungus that grows on rye grass. It was mixed with the 'hard yeest of Ale or Beere' and then applied to the afflicted area with a cloth. Both wild and domestic apples are known to contain valuable nutrients, including vitamin C, so that the old saying of 'an apple a day keeps the doctor away' has a certain amount of truth in it.

Most of the customs relating to apples have grown up around the cultivated versions rather than the more elusive wildings, but their roots extend back over many centuries. Wassailing, the practice of singing or making a commotion in apple orchards, was a regular midwinter practice, especially in Devon and Somerset. Sometimes shotguns were fired into the trees, to scare away any evil spirits that might be planning to spoil the next season's crop; in Sussex, bands of 'howling boys' were first recorded in 1670 and this custom was still going strong in the 1920s. Often the trees would be hit with sticks and sprinkled with cider or ale, while the revellers sang traditional songs.

> Stand fast, root, bear well, top,
> Pray, good God, send us a howling crop,
> Every twig, apples big, every bough, apples now;
> Hats full, caps full, five bushell sacks full,
> And a little heap under the stairs,
> Hulloa, boys, hulloa, and blow the horn!
>
> TRADITIONAL SUSSEX WASSAILING SONG

Meanwhile, in Cornwall at Allantide, the feast of Saint Allan or Arlan which falls on Halloween, children were given a large red apple to put under their pillows for good luck; older, unmarried recipients hoped to dream of their sweethearts. Sometimes, two pieces of wood were nailed together in the shape of a cross, with candles placed on the 'arms' and apples suspended from them on strings: those taking part in the festivities had to catch the apples in their mouth, dodging the drips of hot wax. After the apples were eaten, the pips still held some significance: in many parts of Britain, lovers would throw an apple pip into the fire and watch to see what happened: if it exploded, their love was true; if it smouldered, it was false.

Several superstitions grew up around the apple trees themselves: in Derbyshire, there was a saying that if the sun shone through the branches on Old Christmas Day (6 January), a good crop could be expected next autumn:

> *If wold Christmas Day be fair and bright*
> *Ye'd have apples to your heart's delight.*

In Huntingdonshire, it was believed that if there was no rain on St Swithin's Day (15 July), the apples would not keep through the winter. And woe betide anyone who saw apple trees flowering out of season, as that fateful sight foretold a death in the family.

In Norse mythology, apples have been associated with immortality; with this in mind, it is tempting to consider the fate of King Arthur, the 'once and future king'. According to legend, after he was wounded at the Battle of Camlann, Arthur was taken to the Isle of Avalon, which in Welsh (Ynys Afallon or Afallach) means 'the isle of apples' or 'the isle of fruit'.

Apple trees also held a significance for Merlin or Myrddin, the 'wild man of the woods' in Geoffrey of Monmouth's twelfth-century Latin poem *Vita Merlini*. Driven mad with grief after his friends are killed in battle, Merlin flees to the woods, but when winter comes he has no food. On seeing the bare trees, he laments: 'Here once there stood nineteen apple trees bearing apples every year; now they are not standing. Who has taken them away from me?'

Merlin is also connected with Afal Ynys Enlli, an old apple tree growing on Bardsey Island off the coast of North Wales. This tree, which is leaning against a house, has been examined by a leading fruit historian and is believed to be one of a kind. Locally, it is called

'Merlin's apple', because the sorcerer is believed to be buried in a glass coffin in a cave on the island. If this is the case, perhaps his spirit has been reunited with the apples he once mourned.

> *The beech is dipped in wine; the shower*
> *Is burnished; on the swinging flower*
> *The latest bee doth sit.*
> *The low Sun stares through dust of gold,*
> *And o'er the darkening heath and wold*
> *The large ghost moth doth flit.*
> *In every orchard Autumn stands,*
> *With apples in his golden hands.*

ALEXANDER SMITH, FROM 'GLASGOW', CITY POEMS (1857)

ASH

Fraxinus excelsior

I have sometimes heard the Oak called
the Hercules of the forest; and the Ash, the Venus.
WILLIAM GILPIN, FROM *REMARKS ON FOREST SCENERY* (1791)

It is exhilarating to watch a large ash tree in high wind, as the gusts sweep through its branches and lift them like sails, spinning the leaves wildly against one another with a noise like waves crashing on a shore.

Ash is common in woodlands and hedgerows throughout Britain, and venerable old specimens can sometimes be found, their latticed bark thickly encrusted with moss and lichen. Although ash trees can live to around 180 years, their lifespan is prolonged considerably by coppicing: a fine example of an ash 'stool' in Bradfield Woods, Suffolk, measures over 18ft (5.5m) in diameter and is reckoned to be more than a thousand years old.

Recognisable in winter from its sooty-black buds borne on long, grey fingers, ash is one of the last trees to come into leaf. 'Oak before ash, there'll be a splash; ash before oak, there'll a soak', is a much-debated prophecy about the summer to come. The leaves consist of between nine and thirteen leaflets, usually longer and less noticeably serrated than those of rowan. Clusters of tiny flowers burst from the black buds; the purplish male flowers release clouds of pollen to fertilise the greenish flowers of the female tree, which ripen into dangling bunches of dry brown fruits known as 'keys'. Ash trees have the ability to change sex from year to year, so that trees that bear keys one year may not do so the next.

Traditional names for the fruits include 'ash chats', 'ash candles', and 'cats and keys'. It was once said that Britain's ash trees produced no keys at all in the summer of 1649, which was the year that Charles I was beheaded, and the absence of seeds in any subsequent year was then taken as a bad omen for the royal family.

In autumn, the ash is one of the first trees to drop its leaves, which turn bright lemon-yellow before falling. This timing, according to the old herbalists, was curiously wound up with its reputed power as a snake-deterrent. 'It is a wonderfull courtesie in nature,' wrote John Gerard, 'that the Ash should floure before the Serpents appeare, and not cast his leaves before they be gon againe.' Adders were said to avoid the morning and evening shadows of the tree; even in fairly recent times, when the roadside verges in Wales were still cut by hand, workmen would sometimes carry 'adder sticks' made of ash. If a serpent was still bold enough to strike, the ash provided an antidote for snake venom. Gerard advised that juice from the leaves could be applied to a bite or drunk with wine to produce the same effect.

The leaves had other properties, too: boiled with vinegar and water, they would stop vomiting if laid on the stomach, and the potion taken internally would 'open the stoppings of the liver and spleen'. Gerard claimed that three or four ash leaves taken in wine each morning would 'make those lean that are fat, and keep them from feeding that begin to wax fat'. Today, the leaves are known to have diuretic and laxative properties, and the keys, if picked while still green, have been eaten as a delicate-tasting salad.

> *Beech wood fires burn bright and clear,*
> *If the logs are kept a year.*
> *Oaken logs burn steadily,*
> *If the wood is old and dry.*
> *But ash dry or ash green,*
> *Makes a fire fit for a queen.*
> TRADITIONAL POEM

As a firewood, ash is second to none, producing little or no smoke and providing ash rich in potash. With its strength and elasticity, the timber was prized for making spears and pikes, ladders, carts and farm implements; John Evelyn extolled its virtue, saying 'in Peace and War it is a wood in highest request'. The pale, close-grained wood also makes beautiful furniture, and it continues to find many uses as hockey sticks, billiard cues, oars and tennis rackets. In Northumberland, ash is still used to make the frame of 'creeves' or traditional lobster pots.

According to Norse legend, an immense tree known as Yggdrasil grows on an island surrounded by ocean and connects the nine worlds

ASH
Keys

of Norse mythology; some interpreters have suggested that Yggdrasil is an ash. In some versions of the legend, a deer feeds on the leaves and the great rivers of the world flow from its antlers. A squirrel carries messages from the serpent in the ocean to an eagle that dwells in the topmost branches. A goat also grazes on the tree, and from her udder springs an endless supply of mead, which is enjoyed by warriors feasting in the Great Hall of Odin.

Three of Ireland's five ancient sacred trees were said to be ash, including the Branching Tree of Uisneach, planted by Fintan the Ancient at the centre of all Ireland, and the Sacred Tree of Creevna, a descendant of which was still standing in the early 1800s. Its wood was said to be a charm against drowning, and families who were about to emigrate to America during the potato famine would shave off a piece for good luck.

Picking ash leaves was a certain cure for warts, as long as the sufferer applied them to the affected area while addressing the tree and making a bargain: 'Ashen tree, Ashen tree, pray buy these warts of me.' In Ireland, it was believed that a newborn baby should be anointed with ash sap and be given its first bath by the warmth of an ash fire. Standing under an ash tree during a thunderstorm, however, was foolhardy in the extreme, as it was known to invite lightning: 'Avoid an ash – it courts a flash.'

In some parts of England, country folk would indulge in the strange practice of creating a 'shrew-ash'. This was achieved by making a small hole in the trunk of an ash tree and burying a live shrew in it, while uttering incantations. The tree was then held to have magical properties, and its leaves and twigs were gathered for healing ailments in humans and cattle. The naturalist Gilbert White knew of a shrew-ash standing near the church in Selborne, Dorset, and another example, which was patronised at least until Victorian times, grew in London's Richmond Park. White also recalled a custom that was practised to heal a weak or 'ruptured' child: the trunk of a young ash tree was split, and the child was passed through the cleft, sometimes on successive mornings at sunrise. The tree was then bound up again, and if its wound healed, it was believed that the child would also recover.

The Welsh word for an ash tree is *onnen*, with *onn* as the plural. A traditional Welsh folk song called 'The Ash Grove' tells of a chieftain who set out to kill his daughter's lover, of whom he disapproved, but his arrow struck his daughter instead:

> *Ym mhalas Llwyn Onn gynt, fe drigai penfedig,*
> *Efe oedd ysgweiar ac arglwydd y wlad …*

> *('In the palace of Ash Grove dwelt a chieftain,*
> *Who was squire and lord of the land …')*

Ash trees have an energising, luminous quality about them, and their open foliage allows many wild flowers to flourish at their feet. In parts of Sussex, people would acknowledge an ash tree and wish it 'good day' when passing. Perhaps it is the tree's helpful, positive attributes, and the fact it helps to drain the land on which it grows, that have given rise to the old valediction: 'May your footfall be by the root of an ash.'

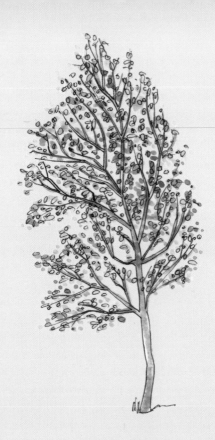

ASPEN

Populus tremula

Feel, masters, how I shake …
Yea, in very truth do I,
an 'twere an aspen leaf …
WILLIAM SHAKESPEARE, FROM *HENRY IV PART II*, ACT II, SCENE IV

A spen must be the only tree that is best distinguished by its voice. In summer, waves of sound spill through its branches, often sweeping from one side to the other, and creating the most beautiful whispering. The leaves have a particularly flexible attachment to the tree, allowing them to flutter and rotate in response to the slightest movement of air; even on a still day, when the leaves on other trees are motionless, an aspen will be dancing to its own secret song.

> *All day and night, save winter, every weather,*
> *Above the inn, the smithy, and the shop,*
> *The aspens at the cross-roads talk together*
> *of rain, until their last leaves fall from the top.*
>
> EDWARD THOMAS, FROM 'ASPENS' (1915)

As one of our native trees, aspen is more common in the north of Britain, where it is an important species in the Caledonian forest. Tolerating a wide variety of soils and climates, it grows at elevations of up to 1,800ft (549m) in the Scottish Highlands, and occurs even in the windswept islands to the north and west.

The aspen's trunk is slender and silvery grey with branches pointing noticeably upwards, as if reaching for the sky. Its leaves are rounded and small, usually only about 1in (2.5cm) across, with lightly notched margins. (Birch leaves can look very similar, but their leaves have a more definite point to the tip.) A fresh bright green in early summer, aspen leaves turn vibrant yellow in autumn, making the tree resemble a tongue of flame. 'One great glory of broad gold pieces appears the aspen,' wrote Arthur Hugh Clough, whose poetry was admired by Queen Victoria.

Catkins are produced in March or April; pollinated female catkins ripen and release tiny seeds. However, in Scotland seed production rarely occurs, for reasons that are not yet properly understood. The aspen has an alternative method of reproduction, however, through suckers or ramets, which spring from its extensive root system.

On the ground beneath an aspen grove the vegetation will often include heather, blaeberry, grasses or bracken, and several species of lichen grow on its bark. Over 60 types of insect feed on its leaves, some of them specifically dependent on the aspen, and in this way it also supports the birds that feed on the insects. Red deer graze on its leaves, and it is a favourite food source for the European beaver.

Aspen wood is flexible and light in weight, making it ideal for use in arrow shafts, and many examples were found on the wreck of the Tudor warship *Mary Rose*. It has been used for lightweight boxes, matches, oars and paddles, and even high-quality paper, but its comparative softness gives it a limited scope for use in building. Although aspen makes good tinder for fire-lighting, and burns with a bright flame, it emits little heat in comparison to oak. In his *Sylva*, however, John Evelyn acknowledged its usefulness: 'Of the aspen our wood-men make hoops, fire-wood, and coals, &c., and of the bark of young trees, in some countries, it serves for candle or torch-wood.'

ASPEN
Leaves

Despite the soft, yielding properties of aspen wood, its Greek name, *aspis*, means 'shield': in Celtic lore it has been suggested that the aspen offered courage to warriors in battle and protection to the spirits of the fallen on their way to the underworld. Like the rowan, an aspen growing near a house was believed to bring good fortune, while an aspen leaf placed under the tongue was said to promote eloquence. In Ireland, a *fé* or rod of aspen was used by coffin-makers to measure a dead body; it is possible that the choice of wood also represented some ancient reassurance of protection to the soul of the deceased. For fishing or farming implements, however, there was a superstition against the use of aspen wood – a sign, perhaps, of its importance.

The leaves, buds and inner bark of aspen contain glucosides called populin and salicin, which act as natural anti-inflammatory agents; in the nineteenth century this knowledge led to the development of aspirin as a painkiller. The healing properties of aspen were known for many centuries before this, however: aspen leaves steeped in water produced a pain-relieving 'tea', while the buds placed in a jar with olive oil created a balm to treat burns, irritations, cuts and scratches. Bitter tisanes made from the bark and leaves were used to treat mild urinary tract infections, and also to alleviate joint pain, sciatica and neuralgia.

> *Like the rowan, an aspen growing near a house was believed to bring good fortune*

In *Plant Lore, Legends and Lyrics* (1884), Richard Folkard describes a 'superstitious practice' used by witches to treat ague or fever: 'A piece of the nail of each of the patient's fingers and toes, and a bit of hair from the nape of the neck, being cut whilst the patient was asleep, the whole were wrapped up in paper, and the ague which they represented was put into a hole in an Aspen tree, and left there, when by degrees the ague would quit the patient's body.'

The aspen's long-held status as a tree of protection and healing suffered a severe setback with the arrival of Christianity. In common with other species, including the holly and the oak, it was believed by some people to have supplied the wood for the cross on which Christ was crucified; the tree's restless trembling was said to denote shame. In the Scottish Highlands there was a tradition of 'dressing down' or berating aspen trees on Good Friday, and stones were even thrown at them; they came to represent bad luck, and their gossiping leaves were denounced as 'old wives' tongues'.

> ... the blessed cross, whereon
> The meek Redeemer bow'd his head to death
> Was framed of aspen wood; and since that hour
> Through all its race the pale tree hath sent down
> A thrilling consciousness, a secret awe
> Making them tremulous when not a breeze
> Disturbs the airy thistledown, or shakes
> The light lines of the shining gossamer.

FELICIA HEMANS, FROM 'WOOD WALK AND HYMN', *THE POETICAL WORKS* (1836)

Communication seems to be the aspen's special gift, and in the past people have sought messages from the spirit world in the murmuring of its leaves. It is a lovely thought, that the tree whose trembling habit is often used as a metaphor for terror was once believed to offer balm and protection at times of deepest fear. The song of the aspen is joyful and uplifting, inviting us to tread lightly on the Earth and listen to its gentle voice.

BEECH

Fagus sylvatica

Bursting forth with abundant sprays of fresh foliage in spring, arching gracefully with boughs of summer green or autumn gold, or sweeping the winter sky with bare, pliant branches … throughout the year, beech trees are a joy to behold, and have inspired many admirers to pay homage to them through words or art.

*... the most lovely of all forest trees, whether we consider its smooth
rind or bark, its glossy foliage, or graceful pendulous boughs.*

GILBERT WHITE, FROM *THE NATURAL HISTORY OF SELBORNE* (1789)

Pollen records show that beech was one of the later tree species to
arrive in Britain after the last glacial period. A native of southern
England and south Wales, elsewhere it is considered an archaeophyte
or ancient introduction. Today, it is naturalised in Ireland and in
Scotland as far north as Caithness, but in general it dislikes wet,
windy conditions, preferring to put its shallow roots down into well-
drained soils.

Beech is one of Britain's tallest broadleaved trees: in 2018, a
specimen growing in the Derwent Gorge, Derbyshire, was recorded
by the Tree Register as the tallest native tree in Britain, at a dizzying
height of 147ft (45m). Few plants will tolerate the dense shade cast
by beech foliage from early summer onwards. Before the leaves are
fully out, bluebells make the most of the dappled light, but afterwards
only specialities such as the ghost orchid, which is not dependent
upon chlorophyll, can truly thrive. Even in winter, some of the lower
branches retain their leaves, offering shelter for songbirds; for this
reason, beech is a popular choice for hedging.

Both male and female flowers are carried on the same tree. The
female flowers develop into small nuts known as mast, which are
held within a prickly husk, and the nutritious kernels are eaten by
deer, squirrels, dormice and many woodland birds. Early human
settlers would have enjoyed them too: beech mast can be ground to
make flour, and in times of famine, even until recent decades, the
leaves helped to stave off hunger. The old tradition of pannage allows
domestic pigs to roam in beech and oak woods during the autumn,
feeding on the fallen mast and acorns.

Long prized as a firewood, beech produces fine charcoal and ash rich
in potash. The Romans burned beech wood to smelt iron, and in the
medieval period green-tinged 'forest glass' was produced in the Weald

of south-east England from beech ash mixed with sand. In Epping Forest and Burnham Beeches, the trees were pollarded and lopped for firewood to feed the hearths and ovens of London. Pollarding can double the average 250-year lifespan of a beech, meaning that some of these old trees can remember the young Henry VIII.

The Romans were well acquainted with the lovers' tradition of carving initials into a tree; they even had a saying, *Crescunt illae; crescant amores*, meaning 'as these letters grow, so may our love'. Graffiti old and new is associated with beech trees in particular, as the bark preserves the inscriptions well. In the mid-1800s, Joseph Tubb from Dorchester carved an entire self-penned poem onto the trunk of a beech tree, now known as the Poem Tree, at Wittenham Clumps in Oxfordshire. His verses were inspired by his love of the local landscape and its history:

> *... Around this hill the ruthless Danes intrenched*
> *And these fair plains with gory slaughter drench'd*
> *While at our feet where stands that stately tower*
> *In days gone by up rose the Roman power ...*

Beeches seem to stand at the heart of written communication: some scholars believe that the word 'beech' is derived from the Saxon *beoce* or *boc*, which also gives us the word 'book'. Gertrude Clarke Nuttall tells us that beech mast was often called 'buck-mast', and that tablets of beech bark were used for early writing.

As a timber, beech wood is hard, smooth and close-grained and is favoured for furniture, joinery and tools. Spalted beech – wood that has been infected with a fungus – displays dark bands and streaks on a pale cream background, making it especially valuable for woodturners. During the nineteenth century, teams of men called 'bodgers' set up camp in the Chilterns, cutting beech wood for the legs and backs of Windsor chairs (the seats were made of elm). The separate parts were then transported for assembly in High Wycombe.

BEECH
Mast

Beeches were widely planted as ornamental trees, inspiring Victorian writer Richard Jefferies who compared a path through a beech wood to the aisle of a cathedral with tall columns rising on either side. 'There is a continuous Gothic arch of green for miles, beneath which one may drive or walk, as in the aisles of a forest-abbey … here, if anywhere, that order of architecture might have taken its inspiration.' (*The Hills and the Vale*, published posthumously in 1909.)

In Nottinghamshire, children would thread beech nuts onto string to make necklaces. In the seventeenth century, John Evelyn recommended gathering beech leaves before the first frost, because they 'afford the best and easiest mattresses in the world to lay under our quilts instead of straw …' (*Sylva*, 1664). Herbalist Nicholas Culpeper recommended boiling beech leaves to make a poultice for swellings, while tar produced from the bark was used as an antiseptic.

Richard Jefferies compared a path through a beech wood to the aisle of a cathedral with tall columns rising on either side

The tallest beech hedge in the world is at Meikleour in Perthshire. Measuring $^1/_3$ mile (0.5km) long and 120ft (36.5m) high, it was planted in 1745 by local landowner Robert Murray Nairne, a Jacobite sympathiser. Nairne was destined to meet his end the following year on the battlefield of Culloden. To the north-west, in Moidart, seven beech trees were planted in the nineteenth century to commemorate the seven companions who landed with Bonnie Prince Charlie at Glenfinnan, at the start of same Jacobite uprising; five of the original seven trees remain.

Beech trees feature frequently in literature. A beech wood in Berkshire is said to be the inspiration for the Wild Wood in Kenneth Grahame's *The Wind in the Willows*. When J. M. Barrie's Peter Pan escapes from his nursery into Kensington Gardens he believes he is a bird and decides to go to sleep in a weeping beech. In *Ivanhoe*, a novel by Sir Walter Scott set in medieval England, Gurth the swineherd's pigs are in 'no haste to remove themselves from the luxurious banquet of beech-mast and acorns on which they had fattened'.

From the burning midday heat of the open glade, it is delicious to plunge into the greenwood; and few forest trees offer such complete and refreshing shade as the delightful Beech. As we lean with luxurious ease against its spacious bole, soft with mossiness, how refreshing to look up into the heaven of leafiness above – how soothing to listen to the music of the leaves as they make merry in the sunshine!

FRANCIS GEORGE HEATH, FROM *BURNHAM BEECHES* (1879)

BIRCH

Betula spp.

… (most beautiful
Of forest trees, the Lady of the Woods), …

SAMUEL TAYLOR COLERIDGE, FROM 'THE PICTURE, OR THE LOVER'S RESOLUTION'
(*SIBYLLINE LEAVES*, 1817)

41

Throughout the seasons, birch trees soften the landscape with their brush-like branches, capturing a thousand trembling raindrops on a wet winter day, or fluttering against a summer sky with a fleet of tiny green pennants; as autumn frosts start to bite, the leaves transform themselves into a shower of golden jewels, clinging as if by magic to dark twigs that already seem to stand in the old year's shadow.

Three species of birch occur naturally in Britain: the silver birch (*Betula pendula*) and downy birch (*B. pubescens*) are widespread, while the dwarf birch (*B. nana*) is a low-growing inhabitant of the Scottish Highlands. Silver birch, which is identifiable by its beautiful silvery bark and small triangular leaves, hybridises freely with downy birch, whose slightly more rounded leaves are borne on down-covered stalks. The two species grow happily in each other's company, but downy birch is more tolerant of poor soil and wet conditions, flourishing in upland areas and along the rain-soaked Atlantic coast.

BIRCH
Leaves and catkins

One of the early colonisers of our ice-free landscape, birch has found countless uses over successive millennia. In Scotland, birch wood was fashioned into carts, ploughs, harrows, gates, furniture, utensils, and even ropes; the bark was used for tanning leather, while the branches were used as fuel in whisky distilling, and for smoking hams and herrings. Birch brush was gathered for thatching, and in summer it was also used for bedding if heather was scarce. In Lancashire, birch was carved into bobbins, spools and reels for the cotton industry.

Birch is monoecious, bearing male and female catkins on the same tree. A single male catkin can release six million pollen grains, and in September thousands of winged seeds are dispersed by the wind. Birch is known to improve the soil in which it grows, and birch woods are rich in wildlife and flora. Occasionally, trees become infested with the parasitic witches' broom fungus (*Taphrina betulina*) which causes a dense, fuzzy mass of growth in the branches.

The connection with witches is not a coincidence: the traditional broom known as a besom, long recognised as the universal mode of transport for witches, is made from birch branches tied to a hazel handle. But birch also had the ability to drive out malevolent spirits: bundles of birch sticks were used in old ceremonies of 'beating the bounds' of a parish, and in the days of corporal punishment, criminals and schoolboys alike felt the sting of a birch rod.

In some counties, particularly Shropshire and Somerset, birch branches adorned the pews on Whit Sunday. In his *Survey of London* (1598), John Stow described how, on the feast of St John the Baptist (24 June), doors would be garlanded with green birch, lilies, fennel and St John's wort, and oil lamps would be kept burning all night. Birch, he explained, is the special tree of St John. On the same day, a sermon was preached in the quadrangle of Magdalen College, Oxford, which was 'furnished round with a large fence of green boughs, that the meeting might more nearly resemble that of John Baptist in the wilderness.' (*Plant Lore, Legends and Lyrics* by Richard Folkard, 1884.)

Long before Christianity, birch kindling was used for fires to welcome the first sunrise of spring. Birch was associated with fertility and childbirth, and in Wales a birch wreath was given as a token of love. A birch 'switch', when used to herd a barren cow, was thought to encourage pregnancy; if it was a fertile cow, she would bear a healthy calf. Maypoles were traditionally cut from a tall, straight birch, and branches were hung over doorways on Midsummer's Eve.

> *Long before Christianity, birch kindling was used for fires to welcome the first sunrise of spring*

Towards the end of *The Return of the Native* (1878), Thomas Hardy describes the preparation of a maypole in a Wessex village. On the evening before the festival the pole was laid down on a trestle, and women began wreathing it in wild flowers from the top downwards. By sunrise it stood in the middle of the village green, wafting a delicious fragrance into the morning air. 'At the top of the pole were crossed hoops decked with small flowers; beneath these came a milk-white zone of Maybloom; then a zone of bluebells, then of cowslips, then of lilacs, then of ragged-robins, daffodils, and so on, till the lowest stage was reached.'

Birch leaves were well known to herbalists, who used them in infusions to treat gout and rheumatism; it was even claimed they dissolved kidney stones. Dried birch leaves were sometimes laid in the crib of a sickly child in order to bring health and strength. Birch sap, drawn from the trunk in spring, was good for cystitis and urinary tract infections, as well as skin disorders; it was also fermented into beer and wine, and Queen Victoria revealed that birch-sap wine was a favourite drink of Prince Albert. Today, birch sap is still tapped in the traditional manner and used to make refreshing drinks.

A black tar made from birch bark is one of the earliest adhesives known to man. Excavations of Neanderthal sites in Europe have shown that 200,000 years ago, people were gluing stone axe heads to wooden hafts with birch-bark tar. When the body of Ötzi, the Neolithic 'ice man', was uncovered in the Alps, his tools showed traces of birch tar, and he also carried two birch-bark containers. It is believed that Neolithic people also chewed the black viscous substance as a natural antiseptic to treat gum infections. Today, research is ongoing into the properties of betulinic acid, found in birch bark, and its potential for treating cancer.

With its natural resistance to water, birch bark has served as a natural writing 'paper' and it has also been used to build canoes. Gertrude Clarke Nuttall describes the lovely fragrance of a birch wood after rain, and notes that '... strips of the bark will burn with a clear, blue flame, giving a delightful and scented illumination.' (*Trees and How They Grow*, 1913.)

Other names for birch include *beith* (Gaelic), *birk* (Scots), *begh* (Irish), and *bedwen* (Welsh). In 1787, during a tour of the Scottish Highlands, Robert Burns was inspired to pen a tribute to the 'Birks of Aberfeldy':

> *Now Simmer blinks on flowery braes,*
> *And o'er the crystal streamlets plays;*
> *Come let us spend the lightsome days,*
> *In the birks of Aberfeldy.*

('Simmer' = summer)

BLACKTHORN

Prunus spinosa

Into the scented woods we'll go,
And see the blackthorn swim in snow.

MARY WEBB, FROM 'GREEN RAIN', *POEMS AND THE SPRING OF JOY* (1928)

The flush of snow-white blackthorn blossom in the hedgerows is one of the first welcome signs of spring. From its knotty black twigs, a profusion of pure white flowers bursts forth, each bearing a spray of yellow-tipped stamens; these have a delicate fragrance, and attract insects seeking early sources of nectar. The appearance of blackthorn blossom often coincides with a particularly cold spell of weather known traditionally as a 'blackthorn winter', a phenomenon described by Surrey-born journalist William Cobbett in 1825:

> It is a remarkable fact that there is always, that is every year of our lives, a spell of cold and angry weather just at the time this hardy little tree is in bloom. The country people call it the Black Thorn winter and thus it has been called, I dare say, by all the inhabitants of this island, from generation to generation, for a thousand years.
>
> THE WOODLANDS

Despite the inclement weather, a blackthorn hedge decked in blossom was traditionally a farmer's call to action: 'When the sloe tree is as white as a sheet,' so the old saying goes, 'sow your barley, whether it be dry or wet.' Greatly admired though it was, there was a strong feeling against bringing blackthorn blossom indoors, and in particular it was never taken into church. One exception was for the sweeping of chimneys: in Ireland, a small sloe bush would sometimes be pulled up and down a chimney, in order to clear it of soot.

Greatly admired though it was, there was a strong feeling against bringing blackthorn indoors

Distributed widely across Britain, blackthorn is able to thrive even on the windswept north coast of Scotland and in the Western Isles. It can grow to around 13ft (4m) in height but usually forms a dense, impenetrable shrub, providing valuable shelter for small birds including nightingales and yellowhammers, as well as for seedlings of other tree species such as oak, ash and hazel. Do not imagine, however, that it ever provided comfortable refuge for humans. Its branches are armed with vicious thorns that can puncture a tractor tyre:

... there are none of the spinous shrubs more hardy, none that make a more glorious shew, nor fitter for our defence, competently armed ... for its terrible and almost irresistible spines, able almost to pierce a coat of mail ...

JOHN EVELYN, FROM *SYLVA* (1664)

One of Britain's rarest breeding birds, the red-backed shrike, has learned to make good use of the tree's sharp spines. Prey species, such as small birds and rodents, are caught and impaled on thorns, and soon a convenient 'larder' of ready meals has been created. This habit has earned the red-backed shrike the nickname of 'butcher-bird'.

The leaves of blackthorn emerge after the flowers, and are known to host the larvae of at least 150 insect species, including the swallowtail butterfly. When picked and dried, they have been smoked as a substitute for tobacco, or used to make 'Irish tea'. In *Wayside and Woodland Trees* (1904), Edward Step remembers that in his youth, a regular jibe against the local grocer was that most of his China tea had been grown on blackthorn bushes not far from home.

Although the trunk of blackthorn rarely achieves a large girth, its branches are tough and knotty, and may be carved into bowls, spoons and tool handles. It makes excellent firewood when dried well, although in the medieval Irish poem *Aidedh Ferghusa meic Léide* ('the death of Fergus'), Iubhdán, the king of the fairies, warns against its use:

Deorad draigen dúr; fid nach loiscenn saer
gáirid elta én; tréna chorp cid cael
('The surly blackthorn is a wanderer, and a wood that the artificer burns not;
throughout his body, though it be scanty, birds in their flocks warble.')
STANDISH H. O'GRADY (ED. AND TR.), FROM *SILVA GADELICA* (1892)

BLACKTHORN
Sloes

One of the most famous uses of blackthorn originates in Ireland, where the tree's dense, heavy wood was believed to symbolise ferocity and physical protection. The fighting stick known as a *bata* or *sail éille* (shillelagh) was often fashioned out of blackthorn; if the piece was cut down just below the root, this formed a convenient knobbly handle which served as the head of the stick when used in combat. First of all, the wood had to be cured, either by burying in a dung heap or by smearing with butter or peat and then placing in a chimney. The bark was left on, as it offered additional strength, but the handle was sanded smooth.

I cut a stout black-thorn to banish ghost or goblin ...
D. K. GAVAN, FROM 'ROCKY ROAD TO DUBLIN'

The nineteenth-century Irish song 'Rocky Road to Dublin' tells of a young Irishman's adventures when he embarks on a ship bound for Liverpool. On arrival, he gets into a brawl with some local boys who start taunting him about his homeland. He lets fly with his shillelagh, and soon he is supported in the fray by some lads from Galway. Quotes from the song appear in James Joyce's *Ulysses* (1922).

It is unlikely that the Mayor of Sandwich in Kent ever feels the need to wield his blackthorn staff in self-defence; instead, in a tradition that stretches back at least 600 years, he carries it as a safeguard against evil spells cast by witches. When a new mayor is elected, the Town Sergeant has the duty of selecting a new wand from the blackthorn trees that grow on Sandwich marshes, and preparing it for the presentation ceremony.

A more sinister use of a blackthorn wand was enjoyed by Major Thomas Weir, a Scottish soldier who served under the Marquis of Montrose. Born in 1599, Weir was a passionate Covenanter committed to opposing interference by the Stuart kings in the affairs of the Presbyterian Church of Scotland, but he had a dark side: during a religious service in 1670 he confessed to a string of crimes and occult practices, including incest and witchcraft. He was sentenced to death and burned in Edinburgh's Grassmarket. His curious blackthorn staff, carved with a satyr's head and reputed to have magic powers, was added to the flames. The magical allure of blackthorn still persists: in the world of the boy-wizard Harry Potter, created by J. K. Rowling, blackthorn makes a powerful wand which is best suited to a warrior.

As if to compensate for the more troubling aspects of its character, every autumn blackthorn produces a crop of fruits that have been enjoyed by the very earliest human inhabitants of these islands right down to the present day. The small black berries, or sloes, have a dusky bloom on their skin and are best picked after the first frost. One of their most popular uses is in sloe gin, but they can also be made into jelly to accompany cheese or meat, or combined with cooked apples in a sorbet.

Sloes have been used as remedies for painful gums, kidney stones, and as a general tonic. According to sixteenth-century herbalist John Gerard, the juice of sloes 'doth stop the belly, the lask [diarrhoea] and bloudy flix, the inordinat course of women's terms, and all other issues of bloud in man or woman ...' (*The Herball*, 1597.)

> At length the stir of rural labour's still,
> And Industry her care awhile forgoes;
> When Winter comes in earnest to fulfil
> His yearly task, at bleak November's close,
> And stops the plough, and hides the field in snows;
> When frost locks up the stream in chill delay,
> And mellows on the hedge the jetty sloes,
> For little birds — then Toil hath time for play,
> And nought but threshers' flails awake the dreary day.
>
> JOHN CLARE, FROM 'NOVEMBER', *THE SHEPHERD'S CALENDAR* (1827)

BOX

Buxus sempervirens

Down with the rosemary and bays,
Down with the mistletoe;
Instead of holly now up-raise
The greener box for show.

The holly hitherto did sway;
Let box now domineer,
Until the dancing Easter-day,
Or Easter's eve appear.

Then youthful box, which now hath grace
Your houses to renew,
Grown old, surrender must his place
Unto the crispèd yew.

ROBERT HERRICK, FROM 'CEREMONIES FOR CANDLEMAS EVE' (C. 17TH CENTURY)

The box is not one of our most familiar trees, but among those people who know and recognise its features, it seems to divide opinion quite sharply. The disagreement hinges upon the distinctive aroma of its foliage, which has been likened to the urine of foxes or cats; and since the box is evergreen, the scent never goes away. While some people find this off-putting, others are enchanted by the perpetual shade cast by stands of old box trees, whose heavily scented greenish gloom has a quality of timelessness.

The seventeenth-century horticulturist John Evelyn was a staunch supporter of the box, claiming that the quality of its wood was ample compensation for the odour of its leaves. Therefore, he argued, 'let us furnish our cold and barren Hills and Declivities with this useful Shrub'. In gardens, too, box had a useful purpose, both for hedging and topiary. Evelyn felt that it was '… infinitely to be preferr'd for the bordering of Flower-beds, and Flat Embroideries, to any sweeter less-lasting Shrub …' Britain's reigning monarch, Queen Anne, was not convinced. She might have humoured Evelyn while he was alive, but shortly after his death in 1706 she had all the box hedging removed from the garden at Hampton Court Palace.

Box is fairly easily distinguished by its small, oval, waxy leaves and clusters of greenish-yellow flowers in spring; mature trees may attain a height of around 20ft (6m). Pollen records show that it once grew as far north as the Lake District, but today it is confined mainly to the counties of Kent, Surrey, Buckinghamshire and Gloucestershire, where it favours chalk or limestone ridges. Place names preserve the memory of box woodland, and in some cases it still grows there: Box Hill in Surrey is perhaps the best example, while others include Boxwell in Gloucestershire, Boxley in Kent, Bexington in Dorset, Bix in Oxfordshire, and Bixley in Norfolk. Charcoal made from box wood has been discovered in the remains of Neolithic settlements on the South Downs.

BOX
Leaves and flowers

Box wood is exceptionally dense – in fact, it is the heaviest wood that can be grown in Europe – and it will sink in water. This can perhaps be explained by its extremely slow rate of growth, its branches taking 200 years to reach a diameter of 4in (10cm). Because of its density, box wood allows excellent sound projection for musical instruments. In the late Baroque and early Classical period, a single-reed instrument called the chalumeau was made from box, as was the later English flageolet.

The pale yellow wood of box has long been popular for furniture inlays, and for making chess pieces, rulers, rolling pins, bobbins for lace-making, nutcrackers, weavers' shuttles, combs and hair ornaments. Nit combs made from box wood were discovered on the wreck of Henry VIII's warship, *Mary Rose*. Exquisite rosary beads or prayer-nuts, intricately carved out of box wood and dating from between 1490 and 1530, can be found in the Waddesdon Collection, originally housed at Waddesdon Manor and now in the British Museum.

Being hard-wearing, box wood is excellent for engraving: the natural history writer and artist Thomas Bewick favoured blocks cut on the end-grain for even greater durability. The popularity of box wood blocks increased so that, during the 1800s, they were widely used for illustrations in *The Penny Magazine* and *The Illustrated London News*.

Box trees became so highly sought-after that they were often sold bit by bit.

In former centuries, box would have been coppiced for firewood and charcoal, but this seems to be a waste of a highly valuable timber. Edward Step, in *Wayside and Woodland Trees* (1904), notes that, when the trees on Box Hill in Surrey were cut down in 1815, the timber realised nearly £10,000 (over £840,000 today).

An interesting custom was preserved until fairly recent times in parts of Lancashire and Cumbria. Before a funeral, sprigs of box were cut and placed on a plate or tray, next to the coffin; mourners were invited to take one and throw it into the grave during the burial service. This practice may have led to the superstition that it was unlucky to bring box into the house at other times: 'Bring box into the house, take a box out.'

'The box is a pleasing object: in winter it harmonises with the ground, and in summer with the woods that surround it'

Hardly surprising, then, that the garden of the manor house in Charles Dickens' *Great Expectations* (1861) has a box tree growing in it. While he waits to see Miss Havisham, the jilted bride who lives in anticipation of her own funeral, Pip stands at the window and gazes over the neglected garden. He sees 'one box-tree that had been clipped round long ago, like a pudding, and had a new growth at the top of it, out of shape and of a different colour, as if that part of the pudding had stuck to the saucepan and got burnt'. Pip's interpretation is playful, but the pervading atmosphere in the house is one of sorrow and neglect.

Still on the theme of sorrow, it is interesting to note that, on Blacklow Hill in Warwickshire, a grove of box and yew trees marks the site where Piers Gaveston, the controversial favourite of Edward II, was executed in 1312.

Oil from box leaves was believed to alleviate toothache, according to John Evelyn, who also claimed that it was an effective treatment for venereal disease. The foliage is poisonous to livestock, however. In his *Herball* of 1597, John Gerard noted that the leaves were not used in medicine and had an 'evill and lothsome' smell.

Writer and clergyman William Gilpin can perhaps be described as the box's most ardently poetic admirer. Describing a walk up to Norbury Park near Dorking, he finds no fault at all with the much-maligned tree, and is all in favour of letting it run riot: 'A regular clipt box wood hedge is an object of deformity: but growing wildly, as it does here, and winding irregularly, at different distances, along the road, it is very ornamental. The box itself also is a pleasing object: in winter it harmonises with the ground, and in summer with the woods that surround it. Box has a mellower, more varied, and more accommodating tint than any evergreen.' (*Observations on the Western Parts of England*).

ALDER BUCKTHORN

Frangula alnus

E asily overlooked in the hedgerow, alder buckthorn is worth a second glance for many reasons, but don't eat the berries! Bright red at first, ripening to purple and then black, they look beautiful, but they are a very powerful purgative.

Described by Carl Linnaeus as *Rhamnus frangula* in 1753, and renamed *Frangula alnus* in 1768 by the Scottish botanist Philip Miller because of its many differences to its close relative, purging buckthorn (*Rhamnus cathartica*), this small-sized tree produces long, straight branches with smooth bark and small, fresh green leaves that may, at first glance, be mistaken for alder – hence the name.

The striking yellowish timber of alder buckthorn once provided the finest charcoal for gunpowder

Also known as breaking buckthorn, black dogwood, butcher's prickwood and berry-bearing alder, its distinctive yellowish wood is hard but brittle; it has been chosen for shoe lasts, butchers' skewers and wooden pegs, while the slender branches can be tied into brooms or woven into baskets. Because of their straightness, they make good walking sticks and are useful in the garden for pea and bean poles, while '… boyes make for themselves arrowes thereof …' (John Gerard, *The Herball*, 1597.)

The striking yellowish timber of alder buckthorn once provided the finest charcoal for gunpowder; it was planted close to gunpowder mills, many of which were owned by the family of horticulturist John Evelyn in Surrey. The light, flammable charcoal was still much in demand for fuses during the Second World War, when the Women's Timber Corps was assigned to seek out natural stands of it in the countryside. To supplement wild resources, alder buckthorn trees were planted in the New Forest and at Wicken Fen in Cambridgeshire.

A deciduous tree, alder buckthorn grows widely across England and Wales, reaching heights of up to 20ft (6m); it prefers damp, peaty

ALDER BUCKTHORN
Berries

soils and can often be found on river banks, sharing its habitat with alder trees. In view of the alder buckthorn's yellowish wood, it seems fitting that one of our most striking yellow butterflies, the brimstone (*Gonepteryx rhamni*), lays its eggs on its leaves. The brimstone will also visit purging buckthorn for the same purpose.

Calico printers once used the green dye that comes from the unripe berries of alder buckthorn; the ripe berries produce a dark blue-grey colour, while a yellow dye can be obtained from the bark and leaves.

Although the berries should be avoided, the bark has been used medicinally as a gentle laxative since medieval times. Traditionally it is collected in summer, then dried for at least 12 months before use. Failure to do this will result in a much stronger purgative. John Gerard, who calls alder buckthorn the 'blacke Aller Tree', does not mince his words:

The inner barke hereof is used of divers countrymen, who drinke the
infusion therof when they would be purged: it purges thick flegmatick
humors and also cholerick, not only by the stoole, but oft times
also by vomit, not without great trouble and paine to the stomack:
it is therfore a medicine more fit for clownes than for civil people,
and rather for those that feed grossely, than for dainty people.

THE HERBALL (1597)

The dried bark, advises Gerard, is gentler in its action; it is also an
effective lotion for toothache when boiled in wine or vinegar, and can
be used to treat 'scabs and filthinesse of the skin'. The leaves, he says,
make good fodder for cattle, encouraging them to produce a good
yield of milk.

PURGING
BUCKTHORN

Rhamnus cathartica

Purging buckthorn, often known simply as buckthorn, is distinguished from alder buckthorn by the presence of thorns, and leaves that grow in opposing pairs, rather than alternately. It tends to prefer calcareous soil, while alder buckthorn favours peaty conditions. The egg-shaped, dark green leaves are finely toothed and glossy, and curl inwards upon themselves along the central vein.

Commonly found in hedgerows, purging buckthorn can reach heights of up to 20ft (6m) if left untrimmed; it is distributed widely across central, southern and eastern England, and is less frequent in south-west England, Wales, Scotland and Ireland. John Gerard, in the late 1500s, discovered that 'it delighteth to grow in rivers and in water ditches ... and in many places more upon the chalkie bankes and hedges.'

Shiny black berries are produced in autumn; like those of alder buckthorn, they are a fierce purgative, and should not be eaten. In 1578 the botanist Henry Lyte advised readers of *A Niewe Herball* that they 'do purge downeward mightily ... with great force, and violence, and excesse', and warned that they should only be administered to 'young strong and lustie people of the Countrie, which do set more store of their money than their lyves'. He continued: 'But for weake fine and tender people, these beries be very dangerous and hurtful, bycause of their strong operation ...' John Gerard, writing in his *Herball* of 1597, advised similar caution, and called the plant by the graphic name of 'laxative Ram'.

Commonly found in hedgerows, purging buckthorn can reach heights of up to 20ft if left untrimmed

Medieval monks, at least those of the Benedictine abbey of St Albans, must have been made of stronger stuff because it appears that they consumed buckthorn berries on a regular basis; whether this was for health reasons or for religious penance it is impossible to know. Evidence was found in the 1920s, when the latrine pits of the monastery were excavated and great numbers of buckthorn seeds were found, alongside scraps of cloth which the monks had used as toilet paper.

Birds seem able to eat the berries with no ill effects, and through their droppings the seeds are widely dispersed. Both purging buckthorn and alder buckthorn are visited by the brimstone butterfly, which lays its delicate, translucent eggs on the leaves. Sheep and deer may browse on the foliage, but cattle will refuse it.

Purging buckthorn is also known as crossthorn, waythorn, hartshorn and ramsthorn; its attractive yellow wood is used by woodworkers for turning and carving. The bark and unripe

PURGING BUCKTHORN
Berries

berries produce a yellow dye for paper, while Gerard describes yet
another use:

There is pressed forth of the ripe berries a juyce, which being boyled with a little
Allum is used of painters for a deepe greene, which they do call Sap-greene.

THE HERBALL (1597)

WILD CHERRY AND BIRD CHERRY

Prunus avium and *Prunus padus*

Loveliest of trees, the cherry now
Is hung with bloom along the bough,
And stands about the woodland ride
Wearing white for Eastertide.

Now, of my threescore years and ten,
Twenty will not come again,
And take from seventy springs a score,
It only leaves me fifty more.

And since to look at things in bloom
Fifty springs are little room,
About the woodlands I will go
To see the cherry hung with snow.

A. E. HOUSMAN, 'A SHROPSHIRE LAD II' (1896)

Few trees can rival the radiant beauty of cherry trees in full bloom: whether they are lighting up an old hedgerow or lacing the edges of mixed woodland, they seem to capture the freshness and exhilaration of spring.

The wild cherry (*Prunus avium*) is naturally widespread throughout Britain and has also been abundantly planted by humans. The bird cherry (*P. padus*) is mostly found in parts of East Anglia, in the hillier regions of northern England, and in Scotland, Wales and north-west Ireland. The two are best distinguished when in flower, as the wild cherry holds its blossom in clusters, with all the stems attached to the twig, while the bird cherry produces panicles of flowers, upright at first and then hanging as the blooms open along a central stem: it is called 'wild lilac' in parts of Yorkshire, probably because of the way it holds its flowers. The wild cherry can reach 100ft (30.5m) in height, while the bird cherry is usually half that size.

The fruits of wild cherry have been enjoyed for millennia, from the earliest inhabitants of Britain right up to the present day.

Archaeologists have found cherry stones in a Bronze Age crannog (man-made island) in County Offaly in Ireland, while in Scotland cherry trees can often be found growing on the sites of abandoned villages. One of the largest wild cherry trees in Britain, with a girth of 21ft (6.4m), can be found on the Studley Royal Estate in Yorkshire.

Bird cherry is also known as hagberry or hackberry in north-east Scotland, where it was often looked upon as a witch's tree and its timber was used only for firewood. Pieces of bark were placed at the door of a house to ward off the plague. The leaves and the bitter black berries or 'hags' contain toxins, but infusions of the bark were once taken as a general tonic, and dyes were extracted from the leaves and fruit.

The fruit of the wild cherry, if it was not eaten raw, was made into preserves or fermented into wine and brandy. It was believed to have plenty of remedial properties: herbalist Nicholas Culpeper advised that the resin dissolved in wine was good for colds and coughs, and claimed that it also improved the colour of the face, sharpened the eyesight, improved the appetite, and helped to break up and expel urinary stones. Henry VIII believed that the fruit eased the pain of gout-ridden joints, and in 1533 he ordered specially bred cultivars of the sour cherry (*P. cerasus*) to be sent from Europe; these were grown in the fruit orchards of Kent. If the guests at his banquets found it difficult to spit the stones out gracefully, they might have agreed that it was best to 'eat peas with the king and cherries with the beggar'!

Bird cherry was often looked upon as a witch's tree and its timber was used only for firewood

Alternative names for the wild cherry include gean (from the French *guigne*), mazzard and merry-tree: 'a cherry year, a merry year' goes the old saying. It was often said that the cuckoo would only stop singing once it had eaten its fill of cherries three times over. This

BIRD CHERRY
Fruit

might be fanciful, but the fruit does provide a summer feast for birds
and small mammals. Then, as the days start to shorten, the leaves turn
glowing shades of amber and crimson so that the tree appears to be lit
from within, and the ground beneath is a sea of burnished gold.

Cherry wood is ideally suited for decorative joinery and cabinet-
making, with an attractive pinkish-brown or honey-coloured
heartwood. It was also used for musical instruments, including pianos
and violin bows, and for beehives. Decking the church with cherry
blossom was an old custom in the Chilterns, where the trees are
abundant, but in some parts of England it was considered an unlucky
flower to have at a wedding.

A good place to see bird cherry is Wayland Wood in Norfolk,
where it grows in the company of hazel, oak, birch, hornbeam and
ash, all amid a profusion of wild flowers. The history of this wood
goes back to the tenth century, and according to local tradition it is
the original setting for *Babes in the Wood*. First published in 1595 in

the form of a ballad by Thomas Millington, this is the tale of two children abandoned in a forest by their wicked uncle.

With its effervescent blooms, the cherry tree was often seen as a manifestation of youthful love and romance. In his poem, 'Cherry-ripe', sixteenth-century composer Thomas Campion describes the face of a beautiful young woman, comparing her mouth to ripe cherries which '… none may buy / Till "Cherry-ripe" themselves do cry'. Shakespeare made frequent reference to the 'cherry lips' of women; in *A Midsummer Night's Dream*, the spellbound Demetrius is enraptured with Helena:

> *O, how ripe in show*
> *Thy lips, those kissing cherries,*
> *tempting grow!*
> A MIDSUMMER NIGHT'S DREAM, ACT III, SCENE II (C. 1595)

The poems of A. E. Housman and Edward Thomas celebrate the transient loveliness of cherry trees but there is also an underlying sense of nostalgia, as if the writer is grasping at time as it slips away:

> *The cherry trees bend over and are shedding*
> *On the old road where all that passed are dead,*
> *Their petals, strewing the grass as for a wedding*
> *This early May morn when there is none to wed.*
> EDWARD THOMAS, 'CHERRY TREES' (POEMS, 1917)

HORSE CHESTNUT

Aesculus hippocastanum

This is the weather the cuckoo likes,
And so do I;
When showers betumble the chestnut spikes,
And nestlings fly ...
THOMAS HARDY, FROM 'WEATHERS', *LATE LYRICS AND EARLIER* (1923)

The horse chestnut is such a familiar and well-loved feature of the British landscape that it is worth remembering that its homeland is the Balkan peninsula, and it has only been growing here for about 400 years. Sources differ as to the exact date of its introduction: Edward Step, writing in 1904, notes that it may have arrived around 1550. It is known that a horse chestnut was growing in the plant collector John Tradescant's London garden in 1633, and in the Scottish Borders a tree called the Union of the Crowns Horse Chestnut is said to have been planted to mark the crowning of James VI of Scotland as King of England in 1603. (This tree was standing until the late 1900s.)

With their majestic stature, massive five-lobed leaves and flamboyant candle-like flowers, the new trees were perfect for ambitious landscaping schemes, and soon they were being planted on a grand scale in large country estates. In 1699, Sir Christopher Wren designed a mile-long (1.6km) avenue at Bushy Park, north of Hampton Court; when Queen Victoria opened Hampton Court to the public, flocks of visitors would gather every year on 'Chestnut Sunday', to promenade and picnic beneath the trees. The custom lapsed during the Second World War but has recently been revived, with an annual parade in May.

Edward Step called the horse chestnut 'the grandest of all flowering trees', but not everybody was convinced about its charms:

The Horse-Chestnut is a heavy, disagreeable tree. It forms its foliage generally in a round mass, with little appearance of those breaks which, we have observed, contribute to give an airiness and lightness … the whole tree together in flower is a glaring object, totally unharmonious, and unpicturesque.

WILLIAM GILPIN, FROM *REMARKS ON FOREST SCENERY* (1791)

John Evelyn, who was usually open to appreciating the values of new trees, was fairly dismissive of its soft timber but wrote that the tree itself '… grows into a good standard, and bears a most glorious flower, even in our cold country …' (*Sylva*, 1664).

72

Evelyn was right about the flowers. Large white panicles appear in May and June, standing upright and giving rise to the colloquial name of 'candle tree'. The leaves can grow to 18in (46cm) across on mature trees, while the bark, pinkish-grey when young, turns a scaly reddish-brown in old age.

> *Large white panicles appear in May and June, standing upright and giving rise to the colloquial name of 'candle-tree'*

The shiny brown fruits are contained within prickly cases, falling from the trees in autumn and littering the ground beneath, to the perennial joy of schoolchildren intent on playing 'conkers'. This game, known in some places as 'conquerors', involves threading the nuts on a short string and engaging in a hand-to-hand battle with a similarly armed opponent, each aiming to hit and smash the other's conker, while (usually!) avoiding the knuckles. It was first recorded on the Isle of Wight in 1848 – surprisingly recent, perhaps, but maybe the earlier trees were inaccessible, being planted on private land. Another name for the contest was 'oblionkers' or 'obblyonkers', referring to a line which had to be recited at top speed by each player before the game:

> *Obli, obli, O,*
> *My first go!*

The first to repeat the phrase was allowed to go first. Flat conkers, often found in pairs, were called 'cheesers' or 'cheese-cutters', while under-ripe ones were known in Yorkshire as 'water-babies'. Since 1965, a World Conker Championship has been held every year on the village green at Ashton in Northamptonshire.

HORSE CHESTNUT
Conkers

Even if you were not inclined to risk your hand at conkers, the simple act of carrying a conker in your pocket was said to prevent rheumatism, and there is a reported case of haemorrhoids being cured with the same method. Neither story can be explained by medical science, but perhaps they perfectly illustrate the power of the mind. Conkers were stored with clothes as moth-repellents, and the saponins – soap-like chemicals – which they contain are sometimes added to shampoos and other toiletries.

During the First World War, Atlantic blockades prevented Britain from importing cordite, a propellant used in the making of ammunition, from North America. The Minister of Munitions, David Lloyd George, knew that cordite was made with acetone, which comes from starch; he worked with Professor Chaim Weizmann of Manchester University to come up with a solution. Weizmann devised a process that extracted acetone from maize and also from conkers. Boy Scouts were promptly set to work and were paid seven shillings and sixpence per hundredweight for bags of conkers, which were delivered to secret factories in Dorset and Norfolk.

The horse chestnut's close-grained, creamy-white wood lacks strength and durability, making it unsuitable for furniture or building purposes, but it is still used for kitchen utensils and small decorative items. As a firewood, it has a tendency to spit out sparks.

It is interesting to ponder the origin of the name 'horse chestnut'. One solution may be that it was considered an inferior version of the sweet or Spanish chestnut, which has similar nuts. However, it seems that in Turkey the conkers were given to horses as a natural remedy for sprains, bruises and other conditions. John Evelyn knew of this use, writing that it was 'so called, for the cure of horses broken-winded, and other cattle of coughs ...' (*Sylva*, 1664). More recently, it has been discovered that aescin, which is extracted from the nuts, has anti-inflammatory properties, validating the centuries-old tradition in its homeland. Maybe the tree knows its own secrets better than anyone: after a leaf has fallen, a horseshoe-shaped scar is left behind on the twig, complete with tiny 'nail holes'.

In Charlotte Brontë's *Jane Eyre* (1847), on a calm summer's evening Mr Rochester proposes marriage to Jane as they sit beneath an old horse chestnut tree. Initially sceptical, Jane passes through a tempest of emotions, from anguish to acceptance and joy; but a storm is brewing, and in the morning Jane hears the rather ominous news that '... the great horse-chestnut at the bottom of the orchard had been struck by lightning in the night, and half of it split away.' One evening she goes to survey the damage and finds the tree cloven in half but still holding firm at the base. As she gazes at the blackened branches, the moon, 'blood-red and half-overcast', momentarily fills the gap between them with light; she addresses the two stricken halves, saying that 'each of you has a comrade to sympathise with him in his decay', little realising that her own life is about to undergo similar turmoil, and that love, like the moonlight, will bring healing.

SWEET CHESTNUT

Castanea sativa

Glory be to God for dappled things –
For skies of couple-colour as a brinded cow;
For rose-moles all in stipple upon trout that swim;
Fresh-firecoal chestnut-falls; finches' wings …
GERARD MANLEY HOPKINS, FROM *PIED BEAUTY* (1877)

Chestnuts roasting over an open fire are one of the pleasures of a traditional Christmas. Eaten while still piping hot, with a little butter or salt, they embody a simple culinary pleasure that has been enjoyed for centuries, from Victorian street vendors right back to the Romans who first introduced them to Britain. Nowadays, many of the chestnuts offered in supermarkets are imported from Europe, but it is still possible to go out and collect your own for a delicious fireside treat.

> *There is probably a smell of roasted chestnuts and other good*
> *comfortable things all the time, for we are telling Winter Stories –*
> *Ghost Stories, or more shame for us – round the Christmas fire.*
> CHARLES DICKENS, FROM *A CHRISTMAS CAROL* (1843)

Sweet chestnut is not related to horse chestnut, although at first glance their nuts appear similar, being a rich mahogany brown and encased in spiny round husks. Only the nuts of the sweet chestnut are edible. An easy way to identify the tree is to check the leaves: sweet chestnut leaves are long and slender, especially on a mature tree, and have a sharply serrated edge with a pointed tip. The unusual, bisexual catkins release pollen into the wind, but the flowers are also pollinated by insects. In autumn, clusters of nuts develop within fiendishly prickly cases, designed to deter predators and equally off-putting to human fingers.

John Evelyn had much to say in their favour, regretting only that they were wasted too often on animals: 'But we give that fruit to our Swine in England, which is amongst the delicaces of Princes in other Countries; and being of the larger Nut, is a lusty, and masculine food for Rustics at all times.' (*Sylva*, 1664.) The monks of Flaxley Abbey in the Forest of Dean certainly enjoyed them, because in the twelfth century King Henry II granted a tithe (tenth share) of the chestnuts in part of the forest.

With its natural homeland in the warmer climates of southern Europe, sweet chestnut only really prospers in the south of Britain, where it is now naturalised. In the woods of Kent and Sussex it has long been coppiced for hop poles, pit props and hoops for barrels. The durable timber is popular for outdoor use, including fencing, seating and window frames; John Evelyn noted that sweet chestnut was used to build many houses of the city of London, which he described as 'ancient' in the seventeenth century. However, the trunks of some mature trees have a tendency to twist, which can cause fissures in the wood, and old trees often become hollow.

Sometimes known by their other name of 'Spanish chestnut', the trees were called 'chesteine' in the Middle Ages. They can be exceptionally long-lived and grow to an enormous girth: ancient chestnut woods can be distinguished by their coppice-stools of varying ages and sizes, some as much as 10ft (3m) across. Incredibly, Britain's oldest specimen was already famous in the reign of King Stephen (1135–54): with a rambling girth of 36ft (11m), and surrounded by a family of saplings and self-rooted branches, the Great Chestnut of Tortworth in Gloucestershire is still alive today, meaning that it must be at least a thousand years old.

Sweet chestnut was used to build many houses of the city of London

In Scotland, two venerable trees may preserve memories of a doomed queen: a chestnut growing by the River North Esk near Dalkeith is believed to have been planted by David Rizzio, the ill-fated secretary and companion of Mary, Queen of Scots, as a token of his love for her, while Queen Mary's Tree in North Lanarkshire was reputedly planted by the queen herself, in 1561.

In old age, the bark of a sweet chestnut can become deeply furrowed and encrusted with burrs and bosses. It is rich in tannin, useful for curing leather, and according to John Gerard it also had significant remedial properties: 'The barke of the Chestnut boyled in wine and drunke, stops the laske [diarrhoea], the bloudy flix, and all other issues of bloud.' (*The Herball*, 1597.)

A paste made from ground chestnuts and honey was considered
a cure for coughs, as was a decoction made from boiling the leaves;
this latter remedy was still being practised in Sussex in the 1940s.
Chestnuts must have been a powerful amulet in themselves, as there
are reports of gypsies carrying some in a small bag to ward off disease.

As ornamental trees, sweet chestnuts were planted to grace the
parks and grounds of many fine houses. In Jane Austen's *Pride and
Prejudice* (1813), when Elizabeth Bennet is touring Derbyshire with
her aunt and uncle, she is invited to Pemberley, the country seat of
Mr Darcy. She discovers a grand mansion, whose windows, 'opening
to the ground, admitted a most refreshing view of the high woody
hills behind the house, and of the beautiful oaks and Spanish chestnuts
which were scattered over the intermediate lawn'.

SWEET CHESTNUT
Chestnuts

THE ARMADA TREE

COUNTY ANTRIM

In May 1588, during the reign of Elizabeth I, Philip II of Spain launched a fleet of ships to attack Britain. The Spanish Armada anchored off Calais in July, whereupon the English fleet sent eight sacrificial 'fire ships' into their midst, and forced them into battle. Some of the escaping Spanish vessels were blown northwards in a storm and were wrecked off the coast of Scotland and Ireland.

According to local tradition, the body of a Spanish sailor from the Armada was washed up on the shore at Ballygally in County Antrim. Kindly locals buried the body in an unmarked grave at St Patrick's Church in Cairncastle. In his pockets, the unknown sailor may have been carrying chestnuts from his homeland – or, at least, this is the possible explanation for a sweet chestnut tree that grew from his grave not long afterwards. Examination of the tree, which is still thriving, shows that it dates from the 1600s, adding plausibility to the story.

DOUGLAS FIR

Pseudotsuga menziesii

With Firs your rising Ground and Mountains fill,
The lofti'st Firs adorn the lofti'st Hill,
From bury'd Cuttings soon such Strength they gain,
That daring Winds and Waves they tempt the Main.

<small>RENÉ RAPIN, FROM *OF GARDENS: A LATIN POEM IN FOUR BOOKS* (1718)</small>

The Douglas fir was first 'discovered' in 1792 at Nootka Sound on Vancouver Island by the naturalist Archibald Menzies. Although Menzies is honoured in the tree's Latin name, its common name pays tribute to botanist David Douglas, who collected seeds in 1824 from specimens on the Columbia River in Washington State. Both men hailed from Perthshire.

Spire-like in form, the Douglas fir has heavy, drooping masses of foliage; up close, the fragrant needles are soft and slender, while the cones point downwards, unlike those of true firs. In its native habitat, Douglas fir is capable of reaching breathtaking heights: in 1897 a 465ft (142m) tree was felled in Washington, and it has been proposed that before logging operations began in the nineteenth century, trees of this height were fairly common.

Pitch from the trunk of Douglas fir treated a range of ailments, from skin irritations to coughs and injured bones

In Britain, Douglas firs grow to less than half that height, but they are still magnificent. Some of the country's tallest trees grow at Ardentinny, on the Cowal peninsula, and in the Gwydyr Forest, North Wales. In Reelig Glen, near Inverness, a grove of Douglas firs represents the largest collection of trees exceeding 180ft (55m) anywhere in Britain. Surviving 'parent trees' from David Douglas's expedition can still be found near Scone in Perthshire.

Douglas firs are widely planted in forestry, providing load-bearing beams for construction and timber for boat-building; the light reddish-brown wood is often chosen for veneers, and makes good arrow shafts. In its homeland, pitch from the trunk of Douglas fir treated a range of ailments, from skin irritations to coughs and injured bones; it was also valuable for binding and caulking canoes. The needles have anti-inflammatory and antiseptic properties: 'fir tip tea', said to ease rheumatism, colds and urinary ailments, is still enjoyed with honey and cinnamon.

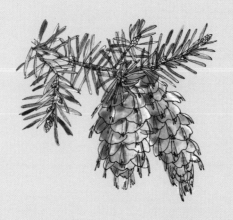

DOUGLAS FIR
Cones

The three-pointed bracts that protrude from each scale of the cone gave rise to a traditional story among America's indigenous people: during a forest fire, so it was said, the mice asked the tree for protection, and their tails and hind legs can still be seen poking out from the cones.

Although David Douglas's legacy lives on, there is an unsolved mystery about his fate: in 1834, while climbing Mauna Kea in Hawaii, he fell into a pit trap and died – either from being crushed by a bull that was already in the pit, or at the hands of a notorious cattle hunter, Ned Gurney, who was the last to see him alive.

ELDER

Sambucus nigra

Garlanded with a froth of creamy blossom in early summer, the elder is found all over Britain and Ireland. With its slender, arching branches and deeply furrowed bark, it prefers to grow on the edge of woodland, in hedgerows or on wasteland, and is an early coloniser of disturbed ground. In remote areas, elder can be an indicator of early human activity, even when archaeological evidence

85

is lost: it loves soil rich in phosphate, which may be present through the accumulation of ashes and animal bones.

Elder leaves are compound, meaning that they consist of individual leaflets – in this case, numbering between five and seven, arranged in opposing pairs with one at the tip. The exuberant blossoms consist of hundreds of individual florets packed tightly together in a large flower head. The flowers emit a heady scent, and are soon buzzing with insects; by autumn, they will have turned to berries that ripen from green to black.

Old names for the elder include 'boontree', 'bottery', 'borewood', 'dog tree', 'ellhorn' and 'ellern'; in Irish it is *trom*, in Welsh *ysgawen*, and in Gaelic *craobh fhearna*. On the Isle of Man, it is known as *tramman*. The word 'elder' is believed to combine the name of the Scandinavian tree-spirit *Hyldemooer* and the Anglo-Saxon word *eldrun*, which comes from *aeld*, meaning 'fire'.

As for the uses of elder – its flowers, leaves, berries and wood – the customs and stories would fill at least one volume on their own. Before any picking or cutting could take place, however, it was essential to ask the permission of the tree. This was not a frivolous practice, but an act of reverence that goes back countless generations. The spirit of the tree was seen as an elderly woman, a mother-figure who possessed powerful magic and could be benevolent or vengeful in equal measure. 'No forester in olden days would dare to cut it down or even lop off a branch, however necessary, without first asking her permission three times over ...' (Gertrude Clarke Nuttall, *Trees and How They Grow*, 1913). For fear of the elder-mother's wrath, no one fashioned furniture from the wood, especially a child's cradle. The hollow branches made good bellows

> *The spirit of the tree was seen as an elderly woman, a mother-figure who possessed powerful magic and could be benevolent or vengeful*

ELDER
Berries

for the flames, but woe betide anyone who actually burned them: the general feeling was that if you did so, you would see the Devil.

The elder's deeply furrowed bark suggests immense age, but in general it is not a long-lived tree. Ancient specimens can sometimes be found, but usually it maintains its presence through seedlings. The pale yellowish timber is exceptionally light, with a fine grain; watch-makers chose it for making tiny components, and it has also been used for fishing floats. The pithy interior of smaller branches can be removed to produce a hollow tube which children eagerly fashioned into whistles and pea-shooters. On the Isle of Colonsay, there is a record of youngsters practising on elder-tree 'chanters' while they were learning to play the bagpipes. As for the pith itself, it has been used for gripping biological specimens while they are examined under a microscope.

No matter how versatile the wood, the flowers and the berries are the most highly prized assets of the elder. The flowers are gathered to make refreshing cordials and wine, and sometimes the entire flower heads are coated in batter and deep-fried to make 'frizzets'. Rich in vitamin C, the berries or 'Englishman's grapes' make delicious wine, as well as jams, jellies and sauces. Elderflower water is valued as a skin cleanser, perhaps with hidden properties: in the Isle of Man, if a girl washed her face in a lotion of elderflowers, it was said to make her more beautiful. Meanwhile, on a more practical level, an infusion of elderflowers in boiling water helps to alleviate piles.

If an elder tree is growing near your house, you can rest assured that you have protection from witches and lightning. But don't go to sleep under it: the strong fragrance of the flowers gave rise to an old saying that 'he who sleeps under an elder tree will never awake'. And beware if there's more than one: stories were told of houses hemmed in by 'the tree of shade and death', whose inhabitants died rapidly and mysteriously. Any survivors apparently recovered miraculously when the trees were felled. It goes without saying that the elder-mother's permission was obtained beforehand.

Belief in the potency of elder trees became so strong in the eleventh century that Wulfstan, Archbishop of York, was moved to forbid any 'vain practices which are carried on waith various spells, and with "frith-splots" [common sanctuaries] and with elders, and also with various other trees ...' (*Ancient Laws and Institutes of England*, Benjamin Thorpe, 1840.)

Wulfstan's warning probably had just as much effect as Cnut ordering the tide to recede. He would have been especially annoyed to know that a cutting from an elder tree growing in consecrated ground was often carried as a charm, and that cross-shaped twigs were especially prized. With its pungent leaves, an elder switch was favoured by cattle drovers to protect their animals from flies, disease, and probably from evil interference, while horse riders would tie a bunch of elder leaves to the horse's harness for the same purpose. Hearse drivers often carried a horse-whip with a handle of elder wood.

Collected and dried, the leaves were used to make tea – named 'ellum blow tea' in the Forest of Dean – and this was consumed as a remedy for coughs, colds and flu. The dried leaves were also smoked as a substitute for tobacco. The seventeenth-century herbalist Nicholas Culpeper claimed that the juice of the leaves 'snuffed up into the nostrils, purges the tunicles of the brain', which is best left as a theory, while in 1597 John Gerard advised sufferers of tumours, swellings or gout to pound the leaves with deer suet or bull's tallow and apply the resulting ointment to the painful area. A hopeful cure for toothache was simply to hold an elder twig in one's mouth and say 'Depart, thou evil spirit!' In a similar vein, scientist and philosopher Francis Bacon in his *Sylva Sylvarum* (1626) advocated the removal of warts by rubbing them with a green elder stick and then 'burying the Sticke to rot in Mucke'.

In north-east Scotland the elder was known as a 'bour-tree':

> *Bour-tree, bour-tree,*
> *Crookit rung,*
> *Never straight and never strong*
> *Ever bush and never tree*
> *Since our Lord was nailed t'ye.*
>
> VERNACULAR SCOTS VERSE
> (CROOKIT RUNG = 'CROOKED WRONG')

Here is one reason why the elder tree has such a mixed reputation, although it is certainly not alone in being accused of providing the cross upon which Christ was crucified. It is also said to be the tree upon which Judas Iscariot hanged himself, and through the weight of shame it is said to be unable to support its own fully grown branches.

In Oxfordshire, a local legend explains the formation of the Rollright Stones, which comprise a Neolithic stone circle and dolmen or burial chamber. As he was marching across the Cotswolds with his knights, a king was challenged by a witch. She told him: 'Seven long

89

strikes shalt thou take and if Long Compton thou canst see, King of England thou shalt be.' To the king's dismay, on the seventh stride a mound rose up and hid Long Compton from view; instantly, he and his men were all turned to stone. The witch transformed herself into an elder tree that is still said to grow in a nearby hedge. If the tree is cut down, her spell will be broken, and the stones will come back to life.

The elder certainly cast its spell over the inveterate wanderer George Borrow, a Norfolk-born author who published several books on his travels through Europe in the 1800s:

Though tall the oak, and firm its stem,
Though far abroad its boughs are spread,
Though high the poplar lifts its head,
I have no song for them.
A theme more bright, more bright would be
The winsome, winsome elder tree,
Beneath whose shade I sit reclin'd;—
It holds a witch within its bark,
A lovely witch who haunts the dark,
And fills with love my mind.

GEORGE BORROW, FROM 'THE ELDER-WITCH', *ROMANTIC BALLADS, TRANSLATED FROM THE DANISH; AND MISCELLANEOUS PIECES* (1826)

ELM

Ulmus spp.

Oh, to be in England
Now that April's there,
And whoever wakes in England
Sees, some morning, unaware,
That the lowest boughs and the brushwood sheaf
Round the elm-tree bole are in tiny leaf,
While the chaffinch sings on the orchard bough
In England – now!

ROBERT BROWNING, FROM 'HOME-THOUGHTS,
FROM ABROAD', *DRAMATIC ROMANCES AND LYRICS* (1845)

91

Those of us who can recall the British countryside before the 1970s might still be able to picture a landscape dotted with elm trees, their upper limbs soaring skywards, the lower branches sometimes shrouding the trunk in foliage almost to the base, giving it a long, recognisably clumpy outline. After the ravages of Dutch elm disease, which killed around 25 million trees over ten years, the elm is no longer as abundant as it once was; but there is cause for hope, as propagation schemes focus on disease-resistant survivors in order to breed new, robust strains of this beautiful tree.

The question of how many different varieties of elm occur in Britain is one that even the most experienced arboriculturists are still debating. The easiest to agree on is the wych elm (*Ulmus glabra*), sometimes known as the mountain elm, Scots elm or (confusingly) wych hazel. A native of the British Isles, it is abundant in upland areas, particularly the north and west of Scotland, and can reach heights of 130ft (40m), even in exposed locations.

Oliver Rackham proposes that, before the Neolithic period, Britain also hosted many kinds of East Anglian or smooth-leaved elm (*U. minor*); English elm (*U. procera*) and Cornish elm (*U. stricta*) may also

ELM
Leaves and fruit in late summer

have been present. Within these main groups, several different types – or, more specifically, clones – exist, and therein lies the key both to the problem of identification, and the elm's particular susceptibility to disease. Although reproduction by seed can sometimes occur, in general the elm puts up suckers from its base, which are genetically identical to the parent tree. This lack of diversity makes the offspring more prone to infection, while the cloning has the potential to throw up a multitude of distinct local forms, making the job of nomenclature something of a challenge.

Also known as the 'elven tree' because it was the haunt of elves, the elm has ancient associations with the underworld and death. Witches were said to avoid them, and since witchcraft was often blamed for the curdling of butter, dairymaids would sometimes put a sprig of elm into the milk churn as a precaution.

The elm's reputation as a witch-repellent is evident in old stories of trial and execution. Until the early 1900s, Maude's Elm in Cheltenham marked the grave of a young girl, wrongly supposed to have committed suicide, and buried with an elm stake through her heart; according to the story, the stake took root and grew into a majestic tree. A similar story surrounds the Beaumont Tree near Silsoe in Bedfordshire, but this elm sprang from the stake driven through the body of a convicted murderer. Until the late nineteenth century, local people suffering from 'ague' would collect their own toenail clippings or strands of hair and pin them to the tree, hoping for a cure. At Brentwood in Essex, Hunter's Elm marked the spot where 19-year-old William Hunter was burnt at the stake in 1555 for refusing to convert to Catholicism.

An old saying warns that 'Elm hateth Man and waiteth', referring to the tree's apparently malevolent tendency to drop branches without warning, even in calm weather. Coffins were often made of elm, but as a firewood it was considered useless:

> *Elm wood burns like churchyard mould,*
> *Even the very flames are cold.*
> FROM A TRADITIONAL POEM

It is tempting to believe that elm trees have an obsession with death! They were certainly no respecter of holy places, often sending suckers under a church if it was growing close by: in the late nineteenth century in Ross-on-Wye, some young elm trees were reported growing inside the church itself.

At Lichfield Cathedral, elm played a part in an age-old ceremony that took place on Ascension Day. Twigs were carried in the procession around Cathedral Close and then placed in the font; according to an old superstition, if the wife of a resident theology student watched this procession, she would conceive a child. Nowadays, the Lichfield choristers place elm twigs above doorways in the Close, but the sprigs carried in the procession are of lime.

In Northamptonshire, the Wicken Love Feast is another Ascension Day tradition, commemorating the union of two parishes in 1587. After morning service, the congregation sings the 100th Psalm beneath an elm tree, before retiring to the parsonage for cake and ale.

For farmers and gardeners, the first flush of elm leaves was a call to action:

> *When the elmen leaf is as big as a mouse's ear,*
> *Then to sow barley never fear;*
> *When the elmen leaf is as big as an ox's eye,*
> *Then says I, 'Hie, boys, Hie!'*
> *When elm leaves are as big as a shilling,*
> *Plant kidney beans, if to plant 'em you're willing;*
> *When elm leaves are as big as a penny,*
> *You must plant kidney beans if you want to have any.*

TRADITIONAL VERSE

With its resistance to decay, elm wood was often used for water pipes: in the seventeenth and eighteenth centuries, several cities, including London, Liverpool, Southampton and Edinburgh, had pipes made of hollowed elm trunks. Elm was used for canal locks and coastal groynes, and for the keels and rudders of ships. Burr elm furniture was greatly admired (a burr is a knobbly mass of shoot and bud tissue that forms wood with an attractive, blurry grain), and in medieval times elm was cut to make the traditional Welsh shortbow.

The nutritious leaves were often fed to cattle, and country folk knew their value in herbal remedies. A decoction of elm leaves was applied to wounds and broken bones, and droplets collected from leaf galls was believed to promote fair skin. Boiled strips of the inner bark were chewed to alleviate colds and sore throats or applied directly to burns. The residue skimmed off water in which elm roots had been boiled was said to restore hair on a bald head.

Elm trees won the affection of poets Sir John Betjeman, William Cowper and Samuel Taylor Coleridge; John Clare's 'The Shepherd's Tree' (*The Rural Muse*, 1835) is dedicated to a wise old elm, while Sir Walter Scott opens *The Lady of the Lake* (1810) with a rallying cry:

> *Harp of the North! That mouldering long hast hung*
> *On the witch-elm that shades St Fillan's spring …*

As the wych elm flourishes in the north of Britain, our embattled lowland trees still hold fast in pockets of the south. Edward Kennion wrote that '… some of the finest parts of England owe much of their beauty to the hedge-row Elms', (*An Essay on Trees in Landscape*, 1844) and in 1912 these beloved sentinels eased the troubled mind of Rupert Brooke as he wandered in spirit across his beloved Cambridgeshire:

> *Say, do the elm-clumps greatly stand*
> *Still guardians of that holy land?*
> FROM 'THE OLD VICARAGE, GRANTCHESTER' (1912)

THE DANCING TREE

MORETONHAMPSTEAD

While most village communities were content with dancing around a maypole on May Day, the inhabitants of Moretonhampstead in Devon went one stage further, and danced in the tree itself.

This was made possible by the shape of a pollarded elm that grew by the market cross; it was known as the Dancing Tree, the Cross Tree or the Punchbowl Tree. The last of these names derives from its proximity to a local inn called The Punchbowl whose proprietor kept it trimmed in an appropriate bowl shape. On festival days, a platform was erected within the boughs of the tree, roped on all sides to prevent people falling off; in 1801, a witness observed that there was enough space on the platform to seat an orchestra and 30 people, while six couples danced. At least one inebriated soul managed to crash through the barriers, landing unconscious on the ground below, but when the alcohol or concussion wore off he was found to be none the worse.

The Dancing Tree has hosted many summertime revellers over the decades, and even offered a meeting place for French soldiers captured during the Napoleonic wars, but it was badly damaged during a storm in 1891 and finally succumbed to another in 1903. In recent years, a rowan tree has been planted in its place.

HAWTHORN

Crataegus monogyna

In hawthorn-time the heart grows light,
The world is sweet in sound and sight,
Glad thoughts and birds take flower and flight.
A. C. SWINBURNE, FROM *THE TALE OF BALEN* (1896)

Old names for hawthorn include quickthorn, whitethorn, hagthorn and mayflower; the berries or haws were sometimes known as 'hog-hazels' and 'peggles'. But there are even more traditions connected with the hawthorn than there are names, because this tree has a very special place in our affections and our folklore.

Britain hosts two native species of hawthorn: the common hawthorn (*Crataegus monogyna*) which is abundant and widespread, and the Midland hawthorn (*C. laevigata*) which occurs in central and southern England. Hawthorn is deciduous and usually forms a compact shape, with small, toothed leaves that are among the first to appear in spring. Pearl-like buds open into five-petalled flowers with a starburst of pink-tipped stamens at their heart. With its dense cover and sharp spines, hawthorn offers protection for a wide variety of nesting birds, and in autumn the small red berries are an important source of food.

More than any other tree, the hawthorn has helped to shape the countryside of Britain through its use in hedgerows; even its name comes from the Anglo-Saxon *hagedorn,* meaning 'hedge thorn'. It is interesting to note that the word 'hag', meaning 'witch', may share the same origin: at one time, witches were thought to ride along hedges, which were a visible line between this realm and the next. A hawthorn hedge therefore protected cattle and crops in both a physical and a spiritual sense.

> *And forth goth all the court both most and lest,*
> *To fetch the floures fresh, and braunch and blome,*
> *and namely hauthorn brought both page and grome …*
> GEOFFREY CHAUCER, FROM *THE COURT OF LOVE* (C. 1346)

Traditionally, on the eve of May Day, the young people of a village would go 'a-maying', heading off into the woodlands and reappearing at dawn with armfuls of fragrant hawthorn blossom. This night-time quest often hid another motive, which was to indulge in some outdoor love-making. Symbolically, the May Queen was united with the Green Man at the time when the Earth was at its most potent and fertile; whether the festival was called May Day, Beltane, or *Calan Mai* (in Wales), the essential meaning was the same.

In modern times, hawthorn is rarely in flower by May Day, and with good reason: in 1752, 11 days were 'lost' when we changed from the Julian to the Gregorian calendar, and the dates of all the festivals jumped forward by the same amount of time. The old May Day would have been celebrated on or around 12 May in the new calendar.

While hawthorn boughs were eagerly gathered, there was a widespread superstition against bringing the blossom indoors: breaking this rule invited the sickness or death of a family member. Uprooting an entire tree was even more dangerous, and country people would avoid it at all costs, even when a hawthorn stood defiantly in the path of the plough. Hawthorns were considered to be the abode of fairies and in Ireland were known as 'gentle bushes'; it was once claimed that the failure of the Northern Irish car manufacturer DeLorean was provoked by the digging up of a 'fairy thorn' to make way for a factory.

This deep-rooted respect for hawthorns still persists in many rural areas, backed up by centuries of traditional tales and folklore. A Welsh legend tells how the sorcerer Merlin was trapped inside a hawthorn tree by a witch called Nimue, while on Eildon Hill near Melrose a thirteenth-century Scottish poet named Thomas the Rhymer is reputed to have encountered the Fairy Queen beneath a hawthorn bush from which a cuckoo was calling. Thomas was led away into the Otherworld, and when he returned to the land of mortals he found that he had been away for seven years.

Gnarled old hawthorns often stand as 'guardians' of stone circles and burial cairns, where their presence seems to be an integral part of the ancient landscape; they are also commonly found next to natural

springs and holy wells, and pilgrims would hang items of clothing or
votive offerings on their branches.

> *Gives not the hawthorn-bush a sweeter shade*
> *to shepherds looking on their silly sheep,*
> *Than doth a rich embroider'd canopy*
> *To kings that fear their subjects' treachery?*
> *O yes, it doth; a thousand-fold it doth.*

WILLIAM SHAKESPEARE, FROM *HENRY VI, PART III*, ACT II, SCENE V (C. 1591)

A hawthorn witnessed the rise and fall of kings: in 1485, when
Richard III was killed at the Battle of Bosworth Field, his crown was
found in a nearby hawthorn bush and placed on the head of Henry
Tudor, who proclaimed himself Henry VII. From this incident arose
the old proverb 'Cleave to the crown though it hang on a bush', and
Henry later took the hawthorn tree as his emblem.

HAWTHORN
Berries

Hawthorn is linked with Christ's crown of thorns, and the Glastonbury Thorn in Somerset is an individual tree whose roots – in legend, at least – stretch back into Biblical times. According to tradition, this tree owes its life to Joseph of Arimathea, the man who buried Christ after the crucifixion: when he came to Britain with the Holy Grail, Joseph thrust his staff into the ground on Wearyall Hill, and it instantly took root. The tree was reputed to have divine properties, and flowers twice a year – at Christmas and again in May. Traditionally, a flowering sprig is sent to the reigning monarch at Christmas, to adorn his or her festive table. During the Civil War, Cromwell's troops hacked down the original thorn, but cuttings had been taken and several descendants survive.

The tree was reputed to have divine properties, and flowers twice a year – at Christmas and again in May

In Norfolk, the Hethel Old Thorn or 'Witch of Hethel' is another claimant to the miraculous staff of Joseph of Arimathea. Mentioned in a thirteenth-century charter, and used for centuries as a meeting place, it has now been granted status as a nature reserve in its own right – albeit the country's smallest, at 0.06 of an acre (0.02ha). Meanwhile in Cheshire, children dance around an ancient hawthorn tree in the village of Appleton Thorn, decorating the branches with garlands in an ancient midsummer celebration called the 'Bawming of the Thorn'.

Berries and flowers were harvested to make jellies, wines and liqueurs for the winter larder; in times of hunger, the fresh leaves were picked to fill empty stomachs, giving rise to the old name of 'bread and cheese'. Hawthorn had beneficial properties, too: in 1620, apothecary and herbalist John Parkinson advised that 'The berries or seedes … are generally held to be a singular good remedy against the stone, if the powder of them be given to drinke in wine; the same is also reported to bee good for the Dropsie …' Fruit compotes were taken to ease diarrhoea, while tea made from the leaves or berries was recommended for heart conditions.

Even the dewdrops that formed on hawthorn blossoms were precious. To enhance their beauty, women would bathe their faces in dew collected from May trees, while men washed their hands in the water, believing that they would become more skilled at their craft. On the rare occasions when hawthorn was chopped down – or when the timber was taken from a fallen tree – its attractive wood was popular for veneers, cabinet work and fine engraving.

Several old sayings link hawthorn trees with the weather, or our response to it. 'Cast ne'er a clout 'til May is out', was the sage advice of our grandparents, who would hang on to every 'clout' or item of clothing until May blossom signalled the arrival of warmer weather. 'Many haws, many sloes, many cold toes' warns that a severe winter usually follows an abundant crop of berries.

When the hawthorn bloom too early shows,
We shall still have many snows.

THOMAS THISELTON-DYER, FROM *THE FOLK-LORE OF PLANTS* (1889)

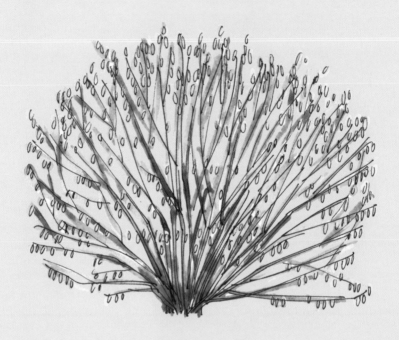

HAZEL

Corylus avellana

J ust after the turn of the year, while the rest of the trees remain dormant and daylight is still fleetingly short, the hazel starts to put forth its catkins. Trembling in the cold wind, these brave little 'lambs' tails' are the first flowers of any tree to appear, and they hold a promise of longer days and warmer sunshine to come.

Widespread throughout Britain, hazel often inhabits the understorey of woodland, but it can also form pure stands, such as Ballachuan Hazelwood in Argyll. This enchanting woodland, with its low canopy and richly diverse flora, is believed to have been in continuous existence since around 7500BC.

Hazel trees are woven into the story of human settlement on our shores. After the last glacial period, they were among the first species to lay claim to the newly exposed earth, and it is likely that their expansion was helped by early settlers who would have carried the nuts with them as a food source. Pits containing hundreds of charred hazel shells, the relics of Mesolithic feasts, have been found by archaeologists on the Scottish islands of Skye and Colonsay; in the Somerset Levels, where trackways across the marsh were laid down from around 4000BC onwards, hurdles of hazel bearing evidence of coppicing are among the first known examples of woodland management in Europe.

For a tree of such long-standing significance, hazel is neither tall nor grand; it rarely grows to more than 40ft (12m), and its trunk is better described as a tightly packed cluster of pale, slender stems which rarely, in old age, meld together. There has been debate about whether hazel deserves to be called a tree at all. Yet in Ireland this was the Tree of Knowledge, and one of the seven noble trees specified in ancient law; Tara, the ancient seat of Irish kings, was located close to a hazel wood, and it was said that members of the *Fianna*, a legendary band of warriors, learned to defend themselves with only a hazel stick and a shield.

According to Irish mythology, nine hazel trees bent their branches over the Well of Wisdom. Their nuts fell into the pool and were eaten by salmon, a fish revered by the druids. The fish developed bright spots on their scales according to how many nuts they had eaten. While cooking one of these salmon for his druid master, a young lad called Fionn mac Cumhaill tasted some of the fish, and thereby absorbed the salmon's magical knowledge. Fionn grew up to become one of the most heroic figures in Irish mythology. To the generations who loved and shared these stories, hazelnuts represented bite-sized wisdom: even today, we speak of concise information contained 'in a nutshell'.

Both male and female flowers are borne on the same tree: male catkins release clouds of pollen to fertilise the tiny red female flowers. The resulting hazelnuts ripen quickly in autumn, to the delight of squirrels, dormice, woodpeckers and jays. Hazel has oval leaves, slightly furry to touch, each with a pronounced drip-tip. Autumn's chill turns them yellow and orange, and beneath this rich canopy have come generations of human foragers, bent on harvesting the rich crop and – apparently – indulging in occasional debauchery. In 1826, for instance, the owner of Hatfield Forest complained about the carousing of men and women from Bishop's Stortford, whose 'nutting' expeditions were opportunities for outrageous behaviour.

Meanwhile, in Thomas Hardy's *Under the Greenwood Tree* (1872), Fancy Day's aspiring lover, Dick Dewy, is infuriated by her flirting and takes himself off into the hazel woods, where he vents his frustration in a frenzied bout of nut-gathering:

At last, when the sun had set, and bunches of nuts could not be distinguished from the leaves which nourished them, he shouldered his bag, containing about two pecks of the finest produce of the wood, and which were about as much use to him as two pecks of stones from the road, and strolled along a bridle-path leading into open ground, whistling as he went.

Although hazel trees have been actively coppiced by man, they are naturally self-coppicing, sending up a host of strong, straight stems which have found a multitude of uses. The young stems are so flexible

HAZEL
Nuts

that they can be tied in knots or bent double, making them ideal for weaving into hurdles and fencing. From Neolithic times, cut hazel was used for wattle, the basis on which wattle-and-daub walls were built, and it is still used to peg down a thatched roof. With their reputation for wisdom, hazel rods were chosen by dowsers, and they were also believed to protect against abduction by fairies. It was said that St Patrick used a rod of hazel to drive all the snakes out of Ireland.

The very name Hazel signifies authority, for when the Anglo-Saxon swineherd cut a supple and stinging twig from the roadside that he might better drive his cattle, he called it his 'haesel' or 'haesl', i.e. his baton of authority.
GERTRUDE CLARKE NUTTALL, FROM *TREES AND HOW THEY GROW* (1913)

Hazel rods are wielded by morris dancers, and they are still used in the curious feudal ceremony of Quit Rent. This is the token payment for a piece of land known as The Moors in Shropshire, whereby two knives – one blunt and one sharp – are presented to the Senior Alderman or the Comptroller and Solicitor of the City of London, who will bend a hazel rod of a cubit's length over both blades. This custom is said to be Britain's oldest surviving ceremony, next to the Coronation. In Abbotts Ann in Hampshire, another fascinating ritual was traditionally performed at the funeral of a virtuous unmarried person of the parish: a 'Virgin's Crown' made of hazel wood, ornamented with paper rosettes and five white gauntlets, was carried in front of the procession by two young girls dressed in white. After the service, it was hung over the West Door so that the congregation could pass beneath it, and if the reputation of the deceased was unchallenged, the crown was then suspended from the roof of the church until it decayed.

> *Nutcrack Night was the joyful evening when the harvest of hazelnuts were first opened*

John Gerard considered that hazelnuts, whether dried or freshly gathered, were hard to digest and 'clogging to the stomacke', although the kernels could be made into a milk which would 'mightily bind the belly' and cool a fever. Today, hazel leaf tea is sometimes used to ease circulatory problems, fevers and diarrhoea.

In many places, Nutcrack Night was the joyful evening when the harvest of hazelnuts, which had been stored away to ripen, were first opened. Then, on the following Sunday, some of these nuts were taken into church and cracked noisily by members of the congregation, perhaps to test the patience of the vicar during the delivery of his sermon. 'Cobnut' is a word that was applied to cultivated hazels, otherwise known as 'filberts' after St Philibert, an early Christian martyr. Filberts from Normandy were widely planted in Kent and became known as 'Kent cobs'.

In his poem 'To Autumn' (1819), Keats imagines the season to be conspiring with the maturing sun:

> '... to swell the gourd, and plump the hazel shells
> With a sweet kernel ...'

While in *Romeo and Juliet*, Mercutio tells Benvolio and Romeo about the enchanting carriage used by Queen Mab, 'the fairies' midwife':

> Her chariot is an empty hazel nut,
> Made by the joiner squirrel or old grub,
> Time out of mind the fairies' coach-makers.
> And in this state she gallops night by night
> Through lovers' brains, and then they dream of love.

WILLIAM SHAKESPEARE, FROM *ROMEO AND JULIET*, ACT I, SCENE IV (1597)

HOLLY

Ilex aquifolium

The holly and the ivy,
When they are both full grown,
Of all the trees that are in the wood,
The holly bears the crown.

TRADITIONAL ENGLISH CAROL

Attracted by its cheerful red berries and glossy green foliage, we have been decorating our homes with holly at midwinter for centuries. Long before the advent of Christianity, holly branches were carried inside during the darkest days of the year, to ward off evil spirits. Later, the green leaves and scarlet berries came to be associated with Christmas; in fact, before the Victorians popularised the idea of bringing a conifer indoors, hollies were known in some counties as 'Christmas trees'.

Although the cutting of boughs for decoration was allowed, the felling of holly trees has always been considered bad luck. Hollies were often left untouched in hedgerows, and it is said that they were used as marker points for farmers when they were ploughing a field. The prickly bushes were thought to stop witches in their tracks, because it was said that witches ran along the tops of hedges.

In Celtic mythology, the holly was linked to the winter solstice: the Holly King was imagined to be a giant covered in holly branches, who ruled during the six months from midsummer to midwinter, before yielding his power to the Oak King. For the Romans, the holly was one of the symbols of Saturnalia, their midwinter festival. To them, it represented immortality, and they gave it to each other as a token of good fortune.

The holly was always considered a masculine plant, with a corresponding feminine presence in the ivy; this belief gives a deeper meaning to the old Yuletide carol, 'The Holly and the Ivy'. In some English villages, midwinter singing contests were held between men and women; the men sang carols praising the qualities of the holly, while the women sang to venerate the ivy. The dispute was resolved under a branch of mistletoe!

Holly has long been believed to protect against lightning strikes, and for this reason it was often planted close to a house. Norse and Celtic cultures associated it with the gods Thor and Taranis respectively (*taran* means 'thunder' in Welsh). Modern science has found a kernel of wisdom in this practice: the spines act as tiny electrical conductors!

The holly bush, a sober lump of green,
Shines through the leafless shrubs all brown and grey,
And smiles at winter be it e'er so keen
With all the leafy luxury of May …
JOHN CLARE, FROM *WINTER WALK* (C. 1832)

Holly is dioecious, meaning that individual trees are either male or female. Flowering occurs on both male and female trees – but only when the tree is about 20 years old. Between May and August small, four-petalled flowers appear, which are a delicate white flushed with pink. Only the female trees will bear berries, and to do so they must be pollinated by a male tree. This job is done mostly by bees, which are attracted by the fragrance of the flowers.

Despite their natural defences, holly leaves are, in fact, extremely nutritious, and the trees were often pollarded by farmers for use as a winter fodder for livestock. The impenetrable holly bush offers a welcome winter shelter for songbirds and provides a safe nesting site in spring. Leaves may stay on the tree for two or three years, and when they fall they take a long time to decay, so that skeleton leaves can often be seen on the ground. The dense leaf litter beneath a holly tree makes a good refuge for hibernating hedgehogs and other wildlife, including toads and slow-worms.

An example of a broadleaved tree that is also evergreen, holly often forms an understorey species in oak and pine woodlands. It dislikes waterlogged conditions, and will not flourish if it suffers prolonged frost: although widespread throughout Britain, it is scarce in Caithness, Orkney, Lewis, Harris and Skye. The New Forest is one of the few places where stands of holly can still be found, and the word 'holm' (holly thicket) occurs in many place names around that region. Further north, the names 'hulver' and 'hollins' have the same meaning.

The Gaelic name for holly, *cuileann*, gives rise to place names such as Cullen in Banffshire and Loch a' Chuilinn in Ross-shire. In Wales, holly is known as *celyn*, and is found in place names such as Bryn Celyn ('hill of holly'), Pentrecelyn ('a village near holly trees') and Coed-y-Celyn ('holly wood').

At country fairs and markets, alcohol was often sold under a holly tree, and it is thought that some pubs called The Holly Tree or The Holly Bush originated in this way. *The Holly-Tree Inn* is the name of a short story by Charles Dickens, set in a Yorkshire tavern of the same name: 'May the green Holly-Tree flourish, striking its roots deep into our English ground, and having its germinating qualities carried by the birds of Heaven all over the world!' (Charles Dickens, *The Holly Tree Inn*, 1899.)

> *The impenetrable holly bush offers a welcome winter shelter for songbirds and provides a safe nesting site in spring*

HOLLY
Berries

Hollies can live up to 250 or 300 years, although some of Britain's oldest specimens, on the Stiperstones in Shropshire, are thought to be over 400 years old. The enduring nature of the holly features in this extract from a song composed by King Henry VIII:

As the holly groweth green
And never changeth hue,
So I am, and ever hath been
Unto my lady true.

FROM 'GREEN GROWETH THE HOLLY', BRITISH LIBRARY ADDITIONAL MS 31922

An infusion of holly leaves has been used as a cure for catarrh, pleurisy and smallpox, and to alleviate the pain of rheumatism. The berries can have violently emetic properties, however, being mildly poisonous. Birds and mammals seem to be immune to these effects, but there is a recorded instance of redwings falling dead out of a holly tree, their crops full of fermenting berries.

Covered in smooth, silvery-green bark, the trunk of an old holly tree can exceed 15in (38cm) in diameter; if left uncut, it may grow to 30ft (9m) in height. The hardwood that it produces is white, with a fine grain; it stains and polishes well, and has been used for marquetry, chess pieces, tool handles and walking sticks. In his *Sylva* of 1664, John Evelyn wrote that 'The timber of the holly … is for all sturdy uses; the Mill-wright, Turner and Engraver prefer it to any other.' Because of its reputation for controlling wayward spirits – including horses – it was chosen by ploughmen and coachmen for use in whip handles.

At Tenbury Wells, on the border between Worcestershire and Shropshire, auctions of holly and mistletoe are held every winter in a custom that stretches back over a hundred years. Branches of holly – berried, unberried, green and variegated – are sent from the surrounding estates and tied in bundles for purchase by florists and other suppliers.

... give me holly, bold and jolly,
Honest, prickly, shining holly;
Pluck me holly leaf and berry
For the day when I make merry.

CHRISTINA ROSSETTI, FROM 'A ROSE HAS THORNS AS WELL AS HONEY', *SING-SONG* (1872)

HORNBEAM

Carpinus betulus

Hornbeam is not one of our most familiar trees, largely because it can be easily mistaken for a beech; but according to pollen records the species has been present in Britain for 5,000 years. It is a native of the south, with a natural distribution ranging from south-east England across to Bristol and parts of south-east Wales; further north, it does occur, but it has usually arrived there with human help.

Our medieval ancestors certainly knew and appreciated hornbeams for their own unique properties. The wood, wrote John Evelyn in his *Sylva* (1664), 'burns like a candle' – and by that, he meant that it burnt reliably, giving out a fierce heat. For centuries, hornbeam trees were coppiced or pollarded for firewood, providing the faggots for bakers' ovens and charcoal for smelting furnaces. Until the mid-1900s, hornbeam logs warmed much of the population of London; even the ash from the fire was valuable, being rich in potash.

Its Latin name *Carpinus* is sometimes said to be derived from *carpentum* (Latin, 'a chariot'), because the Romans fashioned their chariots of its wood (*Trees and How They Grow,* Gertrude Clarke Nuttall, 1913).

'Ironwood', 'hardbeam' and 'yoke-elm' are a few of the old names for hornbeam, referring to the famous hardness and density of its wood. 'Beam' is an old word for a living tree. 'In time it waxeth so hard that the toughnesse and hardnesse of it may be rather compared to horn than unto wood, and therefore it was called Hornbeam or hardbeam,' wrote John Gerard in his *Herball* of 1597. John Evelyn also refers to the tradition that yokes for oxen were made of hornbeam, because it was strong enough to withstand the strain of the plough.

The density of hornbeam was not appreciated quite so fully by woodturners, however. 'The carpenter is not pleased who has hornbeam to work up, for his tools lose their edge far too quickly for his labour to be profitable,' explains Edward Step in *Wayside and Woodland Trees* (1904). Because of the tree's rather unusual habit of creating an oval or irregular-shaped trunk, often deeply fluted and

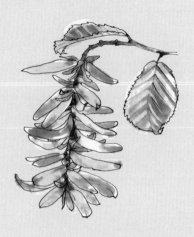

HORNBEAM
Leaves and fruit in autumn

furrowed in old specimens, the timber was of little use for building.
Instead, the beautiful pale cream wood was fashioned – with some
effort – into cogs for windmills and watermills, wheel hubs for carts,
butchers' chopping blocks, billiard cues, skittles, piano actions and
chess pieces.

Before the leaves appear in spring, the tree is decked in dancing
catkins of greenish gold. Both male and female catkins are
carried on the same tree, and after wind pollination the female catkins
develop into green-winged fruits called samaras. These become
brown and paper-dry by autumn and hang in long clusters while the
leaves turn glowing shades of gold. The bark is silvery grey, often
highlighted with wavy streaks in tones of grey or russet, while
the oval leaves are more toothed and furrowed than those of beech.
A variety of witches' broom fungus, *Taphrina carpini*, grows on
the hornbeam, creating clusters of twiggy growth that resemble
birds' nests.

As a natural remedy, a tonic made from hornbeam leaves was said to relieve tiredness, and the leaves were also used as compresses to stop bleeding and help heal wounds. A 'tea' was made from the leaves to soothe symptoms of colds and coughs, and to treat minor digestive problems.

Like the beech, hornbeam creates a dense shade in which most spring flowers – except bluebells and wood anemones – will struggle to grow. A hornbeam hedge will hold on to its dead leaves, providing good winter shelter for small mammals and songbirds. Finches and tits eat the seeds in the autumn, and the tree also provides food and habitat for caterpillars of several moth species, including the nut-tree tussock, autumnal moth and common emerald.

> *Here spiry firs extend their lengthen'd ranks,*
> *There violets blossom on the sunny banks;*
> *Here horn-beam hedges regularly grow,*
> *There hawthorn whitens, and wild roses blow.*

FRANCIS FAWKES, FROM *BRAMHAM PARK – TO ROBERT LANE, ESQ.* (1761)

The ability of hornbeam to create attractive, dense hedges for gardens and labyrinths has long been known to landscapers of stately parks. The maze at Hampton Court Palace is said to have been originally planted with hornbeams, and in Richmond Park an avenue of hornbeams leads to Pembroke Lodge. Another avenue of hornbeams is growing at Anglesey Abbey in Cambridgeshire, planted in 1977 to mark the Silver Jubilee of Queen Elizabeth II.

The Dargavel tree is a vast specimen that stands near Dargavel House at Bishopton in Renfrewshire. One of the largest and oldest of its kind in Scotland, it is thought to have been planted around 1670, and its low, sprawling branches extend over $\frac{1}{3}$ acre (0.1ha). At just over 103ft (31m), the tallest hornbeam in Britain and Ireland stands in the grounds of Mother Shipton's Cave at Knaresborough in North Yorkshire.

119

Trees that have been regularly pollarded or coppiced still develop fantastically contorted trunks in their old age. Around 130 pollarded hornbeams grow in Hatfield Forest, Essex, dating back to the reign of James I; these are now in the care of the National Trust. Many more pollarded specimens can be seen in Epping and Hainault forests.

> *Trees that have been regularly pollarded or coppiced still develop fantastically contorted trunks in their old age*

Gertrude Clarke Nuttall records a particular tradition – and the attempted prevention of it – in Epping Forest. Moved by the poverty of local inhabitants, Queen Elizabeth I gave them permission to cut winter fuel in the forest, on the strict understanding that the lopping must begin at midnight on the night of 11 November. 'Each man who availed himself of her gracious permission had at that hour to strike his axe not less than six feet from the ground into a tree. If he failed to do this he lost the right to the wood.' By the 1800s, royal deer hunting was in decline and the forest was gradually becoming enclosed by the local lords of the manor, who objected to the commoners' long-standing lopping rights. 'Tradition tells the story of one who invited all the potential woodcutters to supper on a certain November 11th and plied them with beer in the hope that they might miss the fateful moment, but in vain. As the midnight hour approached they proved to have kept their wits sufficiently to rise from the supper and go out into the wood.' This old privilege finally disappeared with an Act of Parliament in 1878, which dissolved ancient rights to free lopping; by way of compensation, a public hall, still known as Lopping Hall, was constructed for the benefit of the residents of Loughton, one of the villages on the edge of the forest.

JUNIPER

Juniperus communis

There are three sub-species of common juniper to be found in Britain. *Juniperus communis subsp. communis* is the largest-growing tree, and the most widespread, while *J. communis subsp. nana* is a prostrate form, found in the mountains of northern England, Wales and Scotland. Two small populations of *J. communis subsp. hemisphaerica* can be found growing on the sea cliffs of Cornwall and Pembrokeshire.

These variants mean that juniper in Britain is extremely variable in stature: in less exposed sites in southern England it may reach 30ft (9m) in height, but on the windswept hillsides of western Scotland and the Cairngorms it is low-growing, hugging the contours of the land in the teeth of winter gales. Juniper can creep to higher altitudes than most tree species, venturing up to 3,000ft (914m); at lower levels, it offers valuable cover for nesting birds such as goldcrest, firecrest and black grouse, and its dense prickly mat helps to shelter seedlings of other trees.

At the end of the last glacial period, juniper was one of the early colonisers of grassland; it is scarcer now than it once was, partly through loss of habitat, but thriving colonies can still be found on open moorland, on the edges of woodland, and on chalk downs. Juniper branches are covered with a multitude of needles growing in all directions, and these are so sharp that, in centuries past, it was sometimes cut and placed on top of stone walls in northern England as a substitute for barbed wire. A sprig of juniper was believed to be a potent charm against witchcraft and was often hung above doorways to house and byre during the old festival of Beltane.

At the end of the last glacial period, juniper was one of the early colonisers of grassland

While burning, juniper produces a cedar-like fragrance but comparatively little smoke, a property which made it a favourite fuel for illicit distilling – because, of course, it would not give the secret location away with a tell-tale plume. Inhaling the fumes was said to encourage clairvoyance, and branches were burnt at Halloween to induce contact with the Otherworld. In Scotland, a plague-infected house was fumigated by burning juniper, ideally while the occupants were still inside. Happier uses for juniper smoke include the preparation of food: the smouldering wood gives a delicate taste and aroma to smoked food, including meat and fish.

Old names for juniper include saffern, savin, and (rather confusingly) saffron, although it has no connection with the crocus used to produce saffron spice. In medieval times, giving birth 'under the savin tree' was a euphemistic expression which refers to another of juniper's properties: the berries were known to induce miscarriage in cases of unwanted pregnancy. A sixteenth-century Scottish ballad describes the plight of Mary Hamilton, a fictional lady-in-waiting to a Scottish queen, who has become pregnant by the Queen's husband:

> She's gane to the garden gay,
> To pu' of the savin tree.

(Mary Hamilton was not one of the 'four Maries' who attended Mary, Queen of Scots; there is still some debate both over her identity, and that of the queen.)

In the Pitt Rivers Museum in Oxford is an old artefact consisting of several sprigs of 'saffron' and some accompanying instructions: a woman wanting to end an unwanted pregnancy would soak the leaves in boiling water, allow it to cool, and then drink it every morning for four days. Afterwards, she must place one sprig in each of her boots and wear them for nine days. There was certainly some truth inside this weird custom: until fairly recent decades, juniper pills called 'The Lady's Friend' were advertised in women's magazines.

Juniper was therefore instrumental in preserving a woman's virtue in the eyes of the world, and there does indeed seem to be a long-standing connection between juniper and chastity. Leonardo da Vinci's painting of Ginevra de' Benci (c. 1474) portrays the beautiful young woman with a spray of juniper behind her head. It is believed that the work was commissioned to celebrate her marriage; on the back of the portrait is an emblem with a sprig of juniper and the inscription 'VIRTVTEM FORMA DECORAT' (beauty adorns virtue).

Undeniably, juniper's most valuable assets are its berries. Since it is a conifer, these are actually tiny cones which appear on the female plant and ripen, after fertilisation, to a dusky purplish-grey over a period of three years. They can be ground and used as a peppercorn, and bring a spicy flavour to bread, cakes and sauces. Their remedial properties were well known: 'The berries afford ... one of the most universal remedies in the world, to our crazy Forester. Being swallowed only, instantly appease the wind-collic; and in decoction, they are most sovereign against an inveterate cough.' (John Evelyn, *Sylva*, 1664.)

Juniper berries were recommended for the cleansing of urinary tracts, for dropsy, jaundice, kidney stones, piles, palsy, gout, 'inward imposthumes' (swellings), and the plague. 'The juice of Savin,' advised John Evelyn, 'mixed with milk and honey, is said to be good to expel worms from children,' and it had a similar effect on horses. Nicholas Culpeper went further, claiming that it would 'strengthen the brain' and 'fortify the sight'. Today, juniper is recognised as having anti-inflammatory and antiseptic properties, and the oil is used in perfumery and aromatherapy.

Of the extracted oil, with that of nuts, is made an excellent good varnish for pictures, wood-work, and to preserve polished iron from the rust. The gum is good to rub on parchment or paper to make it bear ink; and the coals, which are made of the wood, endure the longest of any, so as live embers, after being a year covered, have been found in the ashes.

JOHN EVELYN, FROM *SYLVA* (1664)

By far the most popular use for juniper berries was to make gin: in fact, the words 'gin' and 'juniper' share the same source. In the 1800s, juniper berries were harvested in the Scottish Highlands and taken to markets in Inverness and Aberdeen, where they were bought by gin distillers in Holland. In recent years, a number of Scottish distillers have begun offering gin from berries sourced locally in the Highlands and islands.

JUNIPER
Berries

If, having indulged in a couple of gin and tonics on a summer evening, you find yourself dreaming about juniper, pay careful attention to the context ...

> *It is unlucky to dream of the tree itself, especially if the person be sick; but to dream of gathering the berries, if it be in winter, denotes prosperity. To dream of the actual berries signifies that the dreamer will shortly arrive at great honours and become an important person. To the married it foretells the birth of a male child.*
>
> THOMAS THISELTON-DYER, FROM *THE FOLK-LORE OF PLANTS* (1889)

The Gaelic word for juniper, *aittin* or *aiten*, is preserved in some place-names, including Attadale in Wester Ross. In north Oxfordshire, Juniper Hill was the birthplace of Flora Thompson, who immortalised the village in her trilogy, *Lark Rise to Candleford* (1939–43).

LARCH

Larix decidua

Far from being a pioneer of the exposed tundra, or arriving here with the early settlers, larch can trace its British residency back only about 400 years; but in that time, it has become a common and much-loved sight on hillsides and in parkland.

The first specimens of Europe's only deciduous conifer were brought to Britain sometime in the early 1600s. At first, they were known only to a few interested collectors: in 1629, the botanist John Parkinson wrote that the larch was 'rare and nourished up with a few, and those merely lovers of rarities ...' (*Paradisus Terrestris*.) John Evelyn, in 1664, described a specimen growing in Essex as having 'good stature', and went on to warn gardeners not to dig up a larch that had turned brown in autumn, because it was still alive.

Forming a tall, elegant spire when it is allowed free space to grow, the larch has long, tapering branches from which the new shoots are suspended, frond-like, in graceful curves. Needles are held in clusters, and both male and female flowers appear on the same tree: the male flowers are brownish and grow on the underside of the stem, but the female flowers or 'larch roses' are much more flamboyant, being deep vibrant pink; these ripen into papery brown cones.

> *When rosy plumelets tuft the larch,*
> *And rarely pipes the mounted thrush;*
> *Or underneath the barren bush*
> *Flits by the sea-blue bird of March ...*
>
> ALFRED, LORD TENNYSON, FROM *IN MEMORIAM*, VERSE XCI (1849)

Some of the earliest larches recorded in Scotland were brought by the collector Sir James Naesmyth, Laird of Posso and Dawyck, who, according to a report, 'had trees on the brain'. Travelling home from London in 1725 with some young larch trees in his carriage, he stopped to dine with his friend the Laird of Kailzie. Next morning, one larch was planted in Kailzie Park, where it still survives; another was planted at Dawyck, contributing to the establishment of Dawyck Botanic Gardens.

In 1737, when Colonel James Menzies of Culdares, a Jacobite rebel, returned to Scotland after a brief exile abroad, he carried in his portmanteau a number of larches collected in the Austrian Tyrol. He stayed at Monzie Castle near Crieff, where a tree that he planted still stands; it has a girth of over 21ft (6.4m), which is the largest girth for this species in Britain. Menzies then visited James Murray, 2nd Duke of Atholl, at Dunkeld, where he left five larch plants along with other Italian 'exotics'; finally, he returned to his home at Meggernie Castle in Glen Lyon, where the remaining trees were planted.

The Duke of Atholl was delighted when his larches survived, and his enthusiasm for tree planting was passed on to successive generations. The 4th Duke, known as Planter John, believed that planting should be carried out for beauty, effect and profit; his ambition was to supply the entire British navy with larch timber from the Atholl Estates. It is said that cannon loaded with larch seed were fired into areas that were otherwise impossible to reach. By 1830, over

EUROPEAN LARCH
Cones and flowers

14 million larch trees owed their existence to the Planting Dukes, and many other landowners had embraced the cause. One of the very first specimens brought by James Menzies is still alive: known as the Parent Larch, it is growing in the grounds of the Dunkeld House Hotel.

The 4th Duke of Atholl was justified in his belief that larch was good for boat-building, although 'boatskin larch' must be free of knots from an early age, and usually comes from large specimens at least 100 years old. Larch timber, being tough and resilient, is good for all kinds of outdoor use, including fencing, gates and telegraph poles. It is known for its resistance to waterlogging: beneath many buildings in Venice, platforms of larch board support foundation courses of Istrian stone, and John Evelyn mentions the discovery of a larch-built ship which had lain for 1,400 years on the sea bed but 'not one drop of water had soaked into any room.'

One of the very first specimens brought by James Menzies is still alive, known as the Parent Larch

Perhaps because of its relatively recent arrival, there are few traditions attached to the larch in Britain, although the naturalist Gertrude Clarke Nuttall believed that 'the juice of the Larch … was one that the witches used in their potions'. (*Trees and How They Grow*, 1913.) Some sources claim that a decoction of the bark will soothe skin conditions, while infusions of the needles or bark are suggested for treating colds, coughs, bronchitis and urinary infections.

Despite the fact that larch trees bring hillsides alive with colour, first in spring with their vivid green, and then in autumn with a rich golden fire, William Wordsworth could see no beauty in them. 'As a tree,' he wrote, 'it is less than any other pleasing … in autumn, of a spiritless, unvaried yellow; and in winter it is still more lamentably distinguished from every other deciduous tree of the forest, for they seem only to sleep, but the larch appears absolutely dead.' (*A Description of the Scenery of the Lakes in the North of England*, 1810.)

In September 1787, the poet Robert Burns visited the Falls of Bruar in Baluain Wood, Perthshire, and finding the banks bare of trees, he was moved to write a poem which he called 'The Humble Petition of Bruar Water to the Noble Duke of Athole'. In the poem, the river itself is addressing the landowner, inviting him to enhance its setting, because the hot summer sun regularly dries up its waters so that leaping trout are left to wallow 'in gasping death':

> *Would then my noble master please*
> *To grant my highest wishes,*
> *He'll shade my banks wi' tow'ring trees,*
> *And bonnie spreading bushes.*

Unsurprisingly, the tree-loving 4th Duke was delighted to oblige, and soon the falls were planted with overhanging trees, including many larches.

Since the time of the first Planting Dukes, two more types of larch – the Japanese larch (*L. kaempferi*) and hybrid larch (*L. eurolepsis*) – have been widely planted in commercial forestry. The Japanese larch was introduced in the late 1800s, and the hybrid larch arose as a cross-pollination between Japanese and European larches on the Duke of Atholl's estate in Dunkeld.

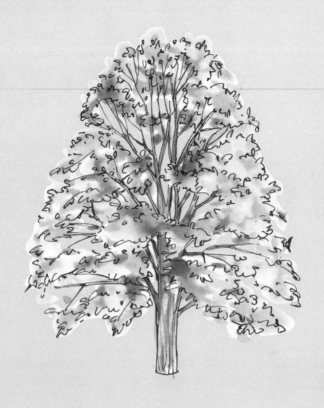

LIME

Tilia spp.

T wo species of lime are native to Britain: the small-leaved lime
(*Tilia cordata*) and broad-leaved lime (*T. platyphyllos*). Together,
they have formed a hybrid, *T.* × *europaea*, or common lime,
which preserves characteristics of both. Capable of reaching 150ft
(45.7m), common limes are among our tallest broadleaved trees and
are widely planted in towns and parks for their stature and beautiful

foliage; in autumn, the ground beneath can be ankle-deep in golden leaves and clusters of tiny globular fruits, attached to the long bracts which act as parachutes to aid their dispersal.

Traditional names for lime include 'linde' or 'linden', and from these arose the shorter versions of 'line' and 'lime'; an old alternative name for the small-leaved lime is 'pry'.

Lime has been present in Britain since about 7300BC. In Suffolk, Norfolk, Lincolnshire, Derbyshire and Herefordshire, fragments remain of ancient lime woods that once extended over much of England and Wales. Native lime becomes scarce from the Lake District and County Durham northwards, and being a relatively slow coloniser it never crossed to Ireland. Memories of lime woods are still preserved in place names such as Lyndhurst, Linwood, Lynsted and Lindfield; Linsty Hall Wood in Cumbria, where limes flourished in the tenth century, preserves the Norse elements *lind* and *stigr*, meaning 'lime path'.

One of the few insect-pollinated trees in Britain, lime waits until June or July to bring forth its small, creamy-yellow flowers which are soon swarming with insects. Bees become intoxicated by the nectar and can often be seen struggling drunkenly on the ground beneath the tree. Linden honey is said to be nutritious and possess medicinal properties, and one of the most fitting uses of lime tree wood is for beehives and honeycomb frames.

> *If thou lookest on a lime leaf*
> *Thou a heart's form will discover;*
> *Therefore are the lindens ever*
> *Chosen seats of each fond lover.*
> HEINRICH HEINE, FROM 'NEW SPRING' (1831)

The leaves of lime are delightfully heart-shaped, and perhaps for this reason the lime tree is known as a meeting place for lovers. In some parts of Europe, scraps of clothing were tied to its branches by women seeking fertility. The thirteenth-century *Völsunga* saga tells the story of the Norse hero Sigurd, who slays the fearful dragon Fafnir and then bathes in its blood so that his skin will become impervious to any weapon. But while he is bathing, a linden leaf falls and lands on his shoulder, protecting that spot from the dragon's blood. Through this vulnerable spot, Sigurd is later killed by the warrior Hagen's spear.

In view of Sigurd's misfortune, it is interesting to note that *lind* in Old English meant 'lime tree' and also 'shield': the wood was chosen by shield makers for its lightness, combined with its ability to absorb a blow. In the Old English epic poem *Beowulf*, warriors are described as *lindhæbbende* – literally, bearers of linden shields. When Beowulf and his band of men arrive on Danish shores intent on killing Grendel, the swamp-dwelling monster who is terrorising Hrothgar's kingdom, they are challenged by a suspicious watchman on the coast: never, he says, have *lindhæbbende* arrived so openly, without the permission (*leafnesword*) of Danish clansmen:

> *No her cuðlicor cuman ongunnon*
> *lindhæbbende; ne ge leafnesword*
> *guðfremmendra gearwe ne wisson,*
> *maga gemedu.*
> FROM *BEOWULF*, 244–76 (c. 10TH CENTURY)

In Shakespeare's *The Tempest*, set on a remote, storm-lashed island, a grove of lime trees surrounds the dwelling of Prospero, the former Duke of Milan. The sprite Ariel assures Prospero that the shipwrecked King of Naples and his followers are being held captive here:

> *All prisoners, sir,*
> *In the lime-grove which*
> *weather-fends your cell.*
> FROM *THE TEMPEST*, ACT V, SCENE I (c. 1610)

133

Centuries later, in his poem 'This Lime-Tree Bower my Prison', the poet Samuel Taylor Coleridge describes himself as another unwilling occupant of a lime grove. Languishing in the shade of the trees, he mourns the departure of his friends who have left him there and continued on their country walk, for reasons which he does not explain. He imagines the lovely scenery that they are exploring, and wishes he was with them; yet the lime tree grove brings a rush of consolation:

> *A delight*
> *Comes sudden on my heart, and I am glad*
> *As I myself were there! Nor in this bower,*
> *This little lime-tree bower, have I not mark'd*
> *Much that has sooth'd me. Pale beneath the blaze*
> *Hung the transparent foliage; and I watch'd*
> *Some broad and sunny leaf, and lov'd to see*
> *The shadow of the leaf and stem above*
> *Dappling its sunshine!*
>
> FROM 'THIS LIME-TREE BOWER MY PRISON' (1797)

The woodcarver Grinling Gibbons (1648–1721) favoured lime for his exquisitely delicate carvings of flowers and fruit, which still grace many churches and stately homes including Hampton Court Palace in Surrey, Chatsworth House in Derbyshire and St Paul's Cathedral in London. To demonstrate his skill, Gibbons even carved a cravat out of lime wood, with a perfectly tied bow and an openwork fall of 'lace'; it was owned by the famous art collector Horace Walpole, who wore it in 1769 when he welcomed distinguished guests to his home at Strawberry Hill, Twickenham. The cravat is now in the Victoria and Albert Museum.

Lime rarely warps, making it an ideal wood for musical instruments and engravers' blocks. Fibres from its trunk have long been harvested into 'bast': in a tradition that stretches back 5,000 years and continued until the last century in some parts of England, bark was stripped off the trees in summer and soaked in water to separate the outer and

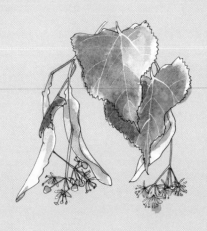

LIME
Leaves and flowers

inner bark. The inner bark was then spun to make cords and rope. The ropes of church bells were traditionally made of lime fibres.

Lime responds well to pollarding and coppicing, and many of the surviving specimens are extremely old. Some stools of lime around Coniston Water in Cumbria are thought to be over 1,000 years old, while at Westonbirt Arboretum in Gloucestershire is a specimen that may be at least twice that age. Now 48ft (14.6m) in diameter, it has formed itself into a circle of individual trees and is still regularly coppiced.

Although it has been flourishing in England for thousands of years, lime is slow to regenerate, especially in the more northerly regions where it rarely produces fertile seed. For ornamental planting, however, lime enjoyed a renaissance in the seventeenth century, when landowners heeded the advice of John Evelyn. The lime, he said, 'will become (of all other) the most proper, and beautiful for walks, as producing an upright body, smooth and even bark, ample leaf, sweet blossom, the delight of bees, and a goodly shade ...' (*Sylva,* 1664.)

Limes were especially popular for planting in avenues: impressive examples still exist at Inveraray Castle, planted around 1650 and possibly the oldest in Scotland; at Kentwell Hall in Suffolk; and at Clumber Park in Nottinghamshire, where the avenue runs for 2 miles (3.2km) and is the longest of its kind in Britain. In Jane Austen's *Emma* (1815), the eponymous heroine, Emma Woodhouse, admires the scenery as she walks around the grounds of Donwell Abbey, the home of Mr Knightley. With her friends, she takes shelter from the sun in 'the delicious shade of a broad short avenue of limes' and concludes that the landscape creates 'a sweet view – sweet to the eye and the mind.'

> *Linden tea, made from either the leaves or the flowers, is still enjoyed as a calming and delicious drink*

Lime has physical benefits, too. Traditionally, the flowers were steeped in hot water to make a fragrant tea called *tilleul* (from its Latin name, *Tilia*); linden tea, made from either the leaves or the flowers, is still enjoyed as a calming and delicious drink. John Gerard's *Herball* of 1597 advises that 'the leaves of *Tilia* boyled in Smithes water with a piece of Allum and a little honey, cure the sores in childrens mouthes'. (Smithes or smith's water was the water into which a blacksmith plunged red-hot iron; once cooled, it was thought to have special healing properties.) Gerard adds that an ointment made with boiled lime leaves, hog's grease, powdered fenugreek and linseed will 'take away hot swellings and bring impostumes [abscesses] to maturation, being applied thereto very hot'.

FIELD MAPLE AND NORWAY MAPLE

Acer campestre and *Acer platanoides*

We seldom see it employed in any nobler service than in filling up its part in a hedge, in company with thorns and briars and other ditch trumpery. Yet the ancients held it in great repute.

WILLIAM GILPIN, FROM *REMARKS ON FOREST SCENERY* (1791)

The field maple is not an outstandingly majestic tree: it does not aspire to any breathtaking heights; nor is it elegant like the beech or the birch, making a more rounded, compact shape than either. It seems, however, that it was much loved by our ancestors, particularly for its wood. A harp made from maple was found in a Saxon barrow at Taplow in Buckinghamshire, and another, wrapped in a sealskin bag, was discovered among the treasure of the Sutton Hoo ship burial in Suffolk.

And while the harpist played, it is possible that a large drinking bowl or 'mazer' was passed around the banqueting table. Often made from burr maple and embellished with precious metals, these mazers held great significance for their owners, ranking among the prized possessions of wealthy families, monasteries and colleges. Sometimes they were given individual names: the Swan Mazer of Corpus Christi College, Cambridge, dates from around 1380; while the late fifteenth-century Chalker Mazer is now held in the Victoria and Albert Museum.

The word 'mazer' has a fascination of its own. The late eighteenth- and early nineteenth-century clergyman and philologist Robert Nares explained that 'it has usually been derived from *maeser*, which in Dutch means maple, or a knot of the maple wood'. Nares points to its occurrence in the work of Edmund Spenser:

> *A Mazer ywrought of the Maple Ware;*
> *Wherein is enchased many a fair sight,*
> *of Bears and Tygers, that maken fierce War:*
> *And over them spred a goodly wild Vine*
> *Entrail'd with a wanton Ivy Twine.*
>
> EDMUND SPENSER, FROM *THE SHEPHEARDES CALENDAR*, 'AUGUST', VERSE 26 (1579)

It is also interesting to note that the words 'mazer' and 'measles' are thought to share the same root, meaning 'spot' – presumably because the markings on the wood were thought to resemble the rash of the infectious disease.

Also called the common or small-leaved maple, field maple occurs throughout lowland England and Wales, but north of the Midlands it is increasingly rare. A native of southern Britain, it is thought to have been introduced to Scotland and Ireland. The distinctive five-lobed leaves turn rich golden yellow in autumn, while

In spring, sap from the bark was collected to make wine and syrup

hundreds of winged fruits or samaras are borne aloft by the wind. In former centuries maples were frequently coppiced and pollarded for their wood, and ancient examples can still be found in Hatfield Forest in Essex. They were also popular for hedging.

Maple wood burns well, and produces good charcoal; in spring, sap from the bark was collected to make wine and syrup. In his *Herball* of 1597, John Gerard claimed that the root, 'pouned and applied, is a singular remedy for the paine of the liver', and translated a Latin verse by the Roman scholar Serenus Sammonicus:

> *Thy harmelesse side if sharpe disease invade,*
> *In hissing water quench a heated stone:*
> *This drinke. Or Maple root in pouder made,*
> *Take off in wine, a present med'cine knowne.*

Richard Folkard, a late nineteenth-century collector of plant lore and customs, noted that, in some parts of England, there was a curious belief that the maple would bless children with longevity if they were passed through its branches. He cites an example in West Grinstead Park in Sussex, where an old maple tree was often used for this purpose, and reveals that villagers raised many petitions of protest on hearing a rumour that it was to be felled.

With excellent sound-producing properties, maple wood is favoured for making musical instruments such as harpsichords, violins and guitars. In the south-west of England, it was much in demand at spring festivals:

'On May-day, in Cornwall, the young men proceed, at daybreak, to the country, and strip the Maple (or Sycamore) trees – there called May-trees – of all their young branches, to make whistles, and with these shrill musical instruments they enliven their way home with "May music".' (*Plant Lore, Legends and Lyrics*, Richard Folkard, 1884.)

The distinctive shape of maple leaves can often be seen carved in medieval churches, for example on the stone pillars of Southwell Minster in Nottinghamshire, where they feature alongside the leaves of other English trees. On 29 April 2011, when Catherine Middleton entered Westminster Abbey to exchange vows with her bridegroom, Prince William, she walked down an aisle that was lined with living field maple and hornbeam trees, decked in fresh green leaves and evoking the essence of the British countryside in spring.

> *The Maple with its tassell flowers of green*
> *That turns to red, a stag horn shapèd seed*
> *Just spreading out its scallopped leaves is seen,*
> *Of yellowish hue yet beautifully green.*
> *Bark ribb'd like corderoy in seamy screed*
> *That farther up the stem is smoother seen,*
> *Where the white hemlock with white umbel flowers*
> *Up each spread stoven to the branches towers*
> *And mossy round the stoven spread dark green*
> *And blotched leaved orchis and the blue-bell flowers –*
> *Thickly they grow and neath the leaves are seen.*
> *I love to see them gemm'd with morning hours.*
> *I love the lone green places where they be*
> *And the sweet clothing of the Maple tree.*
>
> JOHN CLARE, 'THE MAPLE TREE'

Introduced to Britain in the late seventeenth century, and now widely planted in parks and gardens, the Norway maple brings a vivid splash of autumn colour with its brilliant leaves of crimson and gold. Like

FIELD MAPLE
Leaves in autumn

field maple, it has five-lobed leaves, but these have a sharper, more angular outline and finely pointed tips. The pale timber is favoured for furniture and kitchen utensils.

An interesting note on the origin of the word 'maple' occurs in *The Etymology of Plant Names*, a paper read to the Linnean Society by Thomas Comber in 1878. Comber explains that maple is 'a rare instance of a tree-name of the Britons being incorporated into the language of their conquerors the Saxons', passing into early and general use throughout England. As for the derivation, 'it is clearly the Wel. [Welsh] *mapwl*, a knob in the middle of anything, and refers to the knotty excrescence from the trunk of the tree, the *bruscum*, so much employed and so highly valued in the Roman times and in the Middle ages, for making bowls and tables, that single specimens of it have fetched many thousand pounds. The tree was naturally named after its most valuable product, its *mapwl* ...'

BLACK MULBERRY
AND WHITE MULBERRY

Morus nigra and *Morus alba*

It might not be every day that you encounter a mulberry tree, but when you do, it is likely that the experience will leave a lasting impression, simply because of its potential age and heritage.

Neither black nor white mulberry is native to Britain; the homeland of the first is western Asia, and the second hails from China. For centuries, both species have been cultivated in Europe; the white mulberry was especially valued because it is the food plant of the silkworm, which is the larva of the silk moth (*Bombyx mori*).

Black mulberry can grow to a height of 40ft (12.2m), developing a gnarled orange-brown trunk and bearing rough, heart-shaped leaves. White mulberry may be slightly taller with brownish-grey bark, while its leaves are smooth and often lobed. Male and female catkins appear in early summer, on the same tree, and the pollinated female catkins develop into cylindrical drupes or fruits, technically known as a syncarp as it is a conglomerate of several flowers. The ripe fruits, pale pinkish white or deep purplish black, are soft and bruise easily, and perish soon after being picked.

How long have mulberries been grown in Britain? Excavations of Roman settlements close to the Thames have revealed black mulberry seeds, suggesting that they were planted for their fruit; because of their delicate nature, it is unlikely that the berries would have been imported. It is known that black mulberry trees were planted in the gardens of medieval monasteries, possibly for their welcome shade and also for the remedial properties of their fruit, but many old trees were lost during the dissolution of the monasteries under Henry VIII that began in 1536. White mulberry was introduced into Britain in 1596 but has seldom prospered.

During Henry's reign, however, and that of his daughter, Elizabeth I, black mulberries were prized by the nobility for their delicious and exotic fruit. Sir Thomas More, ill-fated Lord Chancellor to Henry VIII, planted mulberries at Beaufort House at Chelsea, and Elizabeth I is thought to have planted a tree in the grounds of Loseley Park near Guildford, home to another More family. In both cases, there was an awareness that *Morus*, the Latin name for mulberry, is also the Latin form of the name 'More'. At Loseley Park the long-standing connection is celebrated with carved mulberry leaves adorning plasterwork and fireplaces, as well as in the family motto, *Morus tarde moriens morum cito moriturum* – 'the mulberry tree is slow to die, while its fruit quickly decays'.

James I and VI, Elizabeth's successor, was inspired to encourage a profitable silk-making industry in Britain. In 1608 he established a mulberry orchard in London and issued an edict to the Lord Lieutenants of the Shires of England to plant a total of 10,000 mulberry trees. Landowners and institutions responded to his challenge: the Cambridge colleges of Emmanuel, Jesus, Christ's and Corpus Christi all planted mulberry trees, some of which still survive. Unfortunately, the King had specified black mulberries instead of white, and the Little Ice Age that had existed from the early

BLACK MULBERRY
Fruit

fourteenth century and continued into the mid-nineteenth century, and brought with it exceptionally cold weather, meant his venture did not enjoy the success he had hoped for.

Several old mulberry trees are linked with great writers. When he entered Christ's College, Cambridge, in 1625, Milton may have sat under the tree in the Fellows' Garden, which is now called 'Milton's Mulberry Tree'. A black mulberry believed to date from the seventeenth century grows in the garden of John Keats's house in Hampstead. Shakespeare was widely reputed to have planted a black mulberry in his garden at New Place, Stratford-upon-Avon, but this tree was felled in the eighteenth century. From its wood, a number of early tourist souvenirs such as snuffboxes and tea caddies were carved, providing a lucrative sideline for woodworkers.

> *The fruit of the mulberry, which was originally white, tradition*
> *tells us became empurpled through human blood ...*
> THOMAS THISELTON-DYER, FROM *THE FOLK-LORE OF PLANTS* (1889)

Pyramus and Thisbe is a story first told in Ovid's epic poem *Metamorphoses* (*c.* 8AD), and features two lovers who meet in secret under a white mulberry tree. Finding traces of blood and wrongly assuming that a lion has killed Thisbe, Pyramus falls on his sword; later, Thisbe returns to find him dead, and stabs herself. The gods, in sympathy, turned the mulberry fruits to the colour of blood. In his comedy *A Midsummer Night's Dream* (*c.* 1595), Shakespeare introduced the story of Pyramus and Thisbe and wove it around his own protagonists, who fall under the spell of a mischievous love potion. Titania, the Queen of the Faeries, becomes enraptured with an actor named Nick Bottom, whose head has been magically transformed into that of a donkey. Hopelessly bewitched, Titania commands her servants to 'Feed him with apricocks and dewberries, / With purple grapes, green figs, / and mulberries.' The story of Pyramus and Thisbe also inspired Shakespeare's *Romeo and Juliet* (1597).

Despite the emphasis on silk production, the timber of mulberry trees was also highly prized, as it turns a rich golden brown with age, and often displays beautiful figuring. It was sought-after for furniture and panelling, and because it was durable it was also used for making hoops and wheels.

With their blood-stained background, it is interesting to note that mulberries were believed by John Gerard to staunch bleeding, and he also recommended them for inflammations of the mouth and jaw.

> *In parts of England, it was believed that the mulberry tree would not come into leaf until the last frosts had passed*

A decoction of bark from the root 'doth open the stoppings of the liver and spleene ... purgeth the belly and driveth forth wormes'. (*The Herball*, 1597.) The same bark, steeped in vinegar, would ease toothache. Until fairly recently, in East Anglia an infusion of mulberry leaves was a traditional treatment for diarrhoea.

Some interesting theories have been put forward to explain the children's song 'Here we go round the mulberry bush'. One proposal claims that it is derived from prisoners taking their daily exercise around a tree in the prison yard. In parts of England, it was believed that the mulberry tree would not come into leaf until the last frosts had passed. The writer Eliza Cook noted this phenomenon in her *Journal*: 'It has, therefore, been called the wisest of trees, and in heraldry it is adopted as an hieroglyphic of wisdom, whose property is to speak and to do all things in opportune season.' (*Eliza Cook's Journal*, 1849.)

For many years, Britain's most successful silk-producing enterprise was located at Lullingstone Castle in Kent, where 20 acres (8ha) of mulberry trees were planted, and 30 rooms of the house were given over to breeding silkworms. Lullingstone produced silk for parachutes during the Second World War, for the coronation robes of Queen

Elizabeth the Queen Mother, and for the wedding and coronation robes of Queen Elizabeth II. Its silk production ended in 2011.

> *The birds such pleasure took*
> *That some would sing, some other in their bills*
> *Would bring him mulberries*
> *and ripe-red cherries;*
> *He fed them with his sight,*
> *they him with berries.*

WILLIAM SHAKESPEARE, FROM *VENUS AND ADONIS* (1593)

OAK

Quercus spp.

'The Druids,' wrote Pliny in the first century AD, '… hold nothing more sacred than mistletoe and a tree on which it is growing, provided it is an oak. Groves of oaks are chosen even for their own sake, and the magicians perform no rites without using the foliage of those trees …'
NATURAL HISTORY, XVI

It is almost as if, ever since oaks began growing in Britain, there have been humans ready to admire them and incorporate them into their most enigmatic ceremonies. For centuries before the Roman occupation, the druids of ancient Celtic culture had been conducting secret rituals amid sacred oak groves, earning themselves such a fearsome reputation that the Romans saw no option but to wipe them out. Their wisdom was lost – and we are left to ponder the tantalising connection between the Welsh words *derwydd*, meaning 'druid', and *derw*, meaning 'oaks': in effect, 'druid' means 'oak wisdom'.

Oak trees were equally revered by the Greeks and Romans. Prospero, in *The Tempest* (*c.* 1610), calls on 'Jove's stout oak', alluding to the oak's connection with the god Jupiter; and in *Coriolanus*, Cominius praises his friend's martial prowess:

> *He proved best man i' the field, and for his meed*
> *Was brow-bound with the oak.*
>
> WILLIAM SHAKESPEARE, FROM *CORIOLANUS*, ACT II, SCENE II (*c.* 1608)

The term 'brow-bound' refers to the tradition that a Roman citizen who saved a human life was crowned with a wreath of oak. Many centuries later, the roles were reversed when an oak tree found itself – quite literally – crowned with a king. Fleeing for their lives after the Battle of Worcester on 3 September 1651, King Charles II and his companion, Colonel Carlos (or Careless), hid in the boughs of an oak tree near Boscobel House in Staffordshire, while a Roundhead patrol passed directly below them. Charles, incidentally, was not unique in his choice of sylvan hideout: Royalist Sir John Rous camped out in a hollow oak for several days while Roundheads occupied his mansion in Henham, Suffolk, his whereabouts known only to his wife who crept out at night to take him food.

Britain's two native species of oak are the English or pedunculate oak (*Quercus robur*) and the sessile oak (*Q. petraea*). Both have leaves of the familiar lobed shape, and both produce acorns; one distinguishing feature is that the English oak carries its acorns on short stalks or peduncles, while the sessile oak's acorns grow directly on the outer twigs. Mature trees can grow to well over 100ft (30.5m) with a massive girth, and the English oak in particular enjoys a lifespan of many centuries. Also known as the 'Durmast' or Welsh oak, sessile oaks are commonest in the north and west of Britain, and are predominant in the ancient oak woods that clad parts of our western coastline. Of all our trees, oaks support the richest fauna, and host an estimated 500 species of invertebrates that are entirely dependent upon them.

Charles II entered London to reclaim his throne on 29 May 1660, which was his 30th birthday. In celebration, he introduced a new annual festival on 29 May, known as Royal Oak Day or Oak Apple Day. This was marked with village parades and dances, and by the wearing of oak sprigs, ideally incorporating an oak apple – a small, marble-like gall which occurs on oak trees and is caused by a gall wasp. Oak Apple Day is still celebrated in a few English counties: a Garland King rides through the streets of Castleton in Derbyshire, covered from head to toe in a cone of flowers, and the church tower is decorated with branches. At St Neot in Cornwall, which was a Royalist parish during the Civil War, a fresh oak branch is put up on the church tower, where it remains for the rest of the year.

Great Wishford in Wiltshire can probably lay claim to the noisiest Oak Apple ceremony. In the early hours, the Rough Band walk through the village, banging dustbin lids, blowing trumpets and shouting 'Grovely, Grovely, Grovely and all Grovely!' This old custom affirms the villagers' rights to collect firewood in nearby Grovely Wood. Oak branches are cut to adorn doorways, and a bough is hoisted onto the church tower; known as the Marriage Bough, it is believed to bring good luck to all couples married that year. Later that day, four women called Nitch Ladies travel to Salisbury Cathedral, dressed in Victorian costume with oak sprigs and bearing a banner featuring the motto 'Unity is Strength'. After dancing on the Cathedral Green, they enter the Cathedral and repeat the cry of 'Grovely, Grovely, Grovely and all Grovely!'

OAK
Acorns

For centuries, oak has provided strong, impermeable timber for the grandest ships and buildings. Henry VIII's warship *Mary Rose* consumed around 1,200 trees in her construction, most of them oaks, and larger ships demanded even more. From the Tudor period onwards, there was also a keen appetite for oak panelling in grand houses. With oak woodlands dwindling, in the seventeenth century John Evelyn was commissioned to produce a discourse on Britain's trees, offering advice to landowners on planting and silviculture. His *Sylva* was published in 1664.

Oak has long been prized by furniture makers, and its bark was valuable in the tanning of leather. Fallen acorns provided rich sustenance for pigs: in the Domesday Book of 1086, woodlands were assessed according to the 'pannage' that they could offer. Oak made excellent charcoal and was burned to smelt iron; the sawdust was, and still is, used in smoking food.

> ... *the rich, high-clustering oak:*
> *King of the woods! whose towering branches trace*
> *Each form of majesty, and line of grace;*
> *Whose giant arms, and high-imbower'd head,*
> *Deep masses round of clustering foliage spread ...*
>
> RICHARD PAYNE KNIGHT, FROM *THE LANDSCAPE* (1794)

One way or another, oak trees seem inextricably linked with Britain's monarchs. In 1100, while hunting in the New Forest, William II was killed by an arrow that glanced off an oak tree; and in Bradgate Park, Leicestershire, a number of curiously flat-headed oak trees are said to have been 'topped' by foresters when the mistress of the park, Lady Jane Grey, was beheaded in 1554. During the Jacobite rebellions from the late seventeenth to the mid-eighteenth century, a sprig of oak carved onto glass and silverware denoted support for the Old Pretender, James Francis Edward Stuart, and later his son, Bonnie Prince Charlie.

Our long-standing affection for 'the king of the woods' is reflected in the fact that we have over 700 individually named oak trees scattered across the country, most of them boasting a story that is stranger than fiction. Some of them have been boundary markers since medieval times, and are still incorporated in Rogation Day ceremonies of 'beating the bounds', when a procession would halt under a 'Gospel oak' to hear a sermon.

Traditional oak remedies include grating a ripe acorn into warm milk to ease diarrhoea and infusing oak leaves in hot water to cure ringworm. In County Donegal in Ireland, water in which oak bark had been boiled was used to treat soreness in horses' shoulders. Offering a recipe that sounds like a witch's brew, John Gerard advises that oak apples should be steeped in white wine vinegar with brimstone and iris root, and the mixture left in the sun for a month; the resulting concoction 'maketh the haire blacke, consumeth proud and superfluous flesh, and taketh away sun-burning, freckles, spots, the morphew [skin disease] with all deformities of the face, being washed therewith'. (*The Herball*, 1597.)

For reasons which we do not fully understand, in some years trees such as oak and beech produce much more fruit than normal. These 'mast years', as they are called, are a widespread phenomenon, occurring throughout the country as if the trees are in some kind of secret agreement to yield a bumper crop. One theory is that over-production of seed may increase the chances of reproduction, since foraging animals cannot eat them all. A rich supply of acorns was certainly a bonus for humans in past centuries, as they were ground into flour for bread-making.

Since at least medieval times, generations of writers and artists have used oak gall ink, derived from the woody growths on oak trees known as oak marble galls. These tiny spheres, caused by the egg-laying activities of a gall wasp, are rich in tannic acid which is extracted and mixed with ferrous sulphate. The resulting brown liquid darkens when applied to paper or parchment, and is very long-lasting, although its acidity often corrodes the writing surface.

In 1798, when he inherited Newstead Abbey in Nottinghamshire, the 11-year-old George Gordon Byron, better known as Lord Byron, planted an oak tree in front of the house, expressing a prophecy that 'as it fares, so will fare my fortunes'. When he visited the house again in 1807 he was alarmed to find the young tree choked with undergrowth, and wrote a poem of encouragement:

> *Oh, live then, my Oak! tow'r aloft from the weeds,*
> *That clog thy young growth, and assist thy decay,*
> *For still in thy bosom are Life's early seeds,*
> *And still may thy branches their beauty display.*
> From 'To an Oak at Newstead Abbey' (1807)

Lord Byron lived a tempestuous life which came to a premature end at the age of 36. The Byron Oak grew to maturity and outlived its namesake by about 100 years.

THE BIRNAM OAK

DUNKELD

On the bank of the River Tay at Dunkeld stands a sessile oak tree which is said to be the last survivor of Great Birnam Wood in Shakespeare's *Macbeth* (1606). In the play, an apparition conjured by three witches warns that 'Macbeth shall never vanquish'd be until / Great Birnam Wood to high Dunsinane Hill / Shall come against him.' Since he is aspiring to seize the throne of Scotland, Macbeth finds this news extremely reassuring, because, as he says himself, 'Who can impress the forest, bid the tree / Unfix his earthbound root?'

After going on a rampage of murder, Macbeth is on the point of achieving his goal: just one more battle stands between him and the crown. But the woods seem to be moving: Malcolm, his opponent, has raised an army and they are heading for Dunsinane, disguised by branches cut from Birnam Wood. Macbeth is panicked into action and is slain by Malcolm.

While the Birnam Oak cannot claim to date back to the eleventh century, the time of the real-life Macbeth, it could have been a mature tree by the late 1500s, when William Shakespeare is rumoured to have visited James VI in Scotland; whether it inspired his play, we shall never know. Far from being a fragile relic, the Birnam Oak stands 90ft (27.4m) tall with vast spreading limbs, and is the picture of robust health.

THE PONTFADOG OAK

CHIRK

Until April 2013, a sessile oak growing on a hillside near Chirk in North Wales was one of the oldest oak trees in Britain, if not in Europe. The Pontfadog Oak was believed to date back to at least 800AD; it would therefore, in theory, remember the arrival of Viking raiders, and the Norman conquest of England; it would witness the rise of Llywelyn Fawr (Llywelyn the Great), and the demise of Llywelyn ap Gruffydd (Llywelyn the Last); in 1165, so it is said, Owain ap Gruffydd, King of Gwynedd and the first Prince of Wales, rallied his forces beneath its branches before clashing with King Henry II's forces in the Battle of Crogen. Another ancient tree, called the Oak at the Gate of the Dead, marks the battle site. Faced with guerrilla tactics, difficult terrain and awful weather, Henry soon abandoned his campaign to conquer Wales.

In later centuries, the Pontfadog Oak, which had been pollarded for timber and firewood, developed stories of its own. Two golden chisels were said to be hidden inside it, and in 1880, six men sat around a table set within its vast hollow trunk. It made a natural playground for children, and eggs would be hidden there on Easter Day. It grew into the hearts of successive generations, so it was a sad day when a gale toppled the tree, just as its leaves were about to burst from the bud. A few saplings, grown from acorns, survive.

WILD PEAR

Pyrus pyraster

When did pear trees first arrive in Britain? The answer to that question is open to debate, but charcoal from pear trees has been found at several Neolithic sites, together with carbonised pips; if they are not a native species, they must have arrived with the first settlers. Several millennia later, pear is the tenth commonest tree species to appear in Anglo-Saxon charters, where individual trees were often used to define boundaries of land. Oliver Rackham, writing in *The History of Countryside* (1986), explains that these pear trees were in remote places, and would not have been orchard trees. He therefore considers these charters to be the earliest written evidence for a tree that is now one of our rarest.

Wild pear (*Pyrus pyraster*) may be distinguished from its cultivated cousin, *P. communis* or common pear, by the spines that it bears, and by the fact that its small, yellowish-green fruits are largely inedible: only when they start to 'blet' or decay do they become soft enough to eat. In spring, a wild pear decked with a froth of white blossom makes a spectacular sight: look for it as an occasional survivor in ancient woodland, such as Hayley Wood in Cambridgeshire and Epping Forest in Essex, and in old hedgerows across southern England and Wales.

In spring, a wild pear decked with a froth of white blossom makes a spectacular sight

Even rarer than the wild pear is the Plymouth pear, *Pyrus cordata*, which exists in the form of a few small, spiny specimens growing in hedgerows in south-west England – particularly around Plymouth, as its name might suggest. In May, Plymouth pear puts forth a profusion of pale cream blossom whose fragrance seems to leave much to be desired: unimpressed wayfarers have compared it to the aroma of rotting scampi or wet carpet. Plymouth pear only grows to about 15ft (4.6m), and as a distinct species it was only identified in 1865. Clusters exist in Brittany, France, and there is still some doubt over whether it is actually a native British tree, or whether it was brought across the Channel, either by human settlers, or in the crops of migratory birds.

Makers of musical instruments such as bassoons, clarinets, flutes, recorders and harpsichords have long favoured pear wood for its pale colour, which is often infused with beautiful pink or reddish hues. When stained black, the wood has been used as a substitute for ebony in the finger-boards of violins. Pear wood makes a fine veneer and lends itself well to small decorative items.

If you have an old pear tree growing in your orchard, it is more likely to be a cultivated variety of *P. communis,* the common pear. Over the centuries, hundreds of different strains have been developed, either for their distinctive fruit or for perry-making: the county of Gloucestershire alone can lay claim to more than 100 types of perry pear. Some of their delightfully irreverent old names include Lumberskull, Merrylegs, Devildrink, Bastard Sack, Mumblehead and Stinking Bishop – a warning, perhaps, of the dangers of over-indulgence!

In the early 1400s pears of a variety called Parkinson's Warden, grown at the Cistercian abbey of Warden in Bedfordshire, were shipped to France for the enjoyment of English soldiers preparing for the Battle of Agincourt. These pears were more than a delicious luxury: they provided an important source of vitamins and were especially valuable because they would keep well for several months.

PLYMOUTH PEAR
Fruit

In Shakespeare's *The Winter's Tale* (*c.* 1609), it is the Warden pear to which the Young Shepherd refers when he declares: 'I must have saffron / to colour the warden pies.' (Act IV, Scene III.)

The branches of a pear tree seem an unlikely setting for a lovers' tryst, but two of Chaucer's characters find them surprisingly comfortable and convenient. In *The Merchant's Tale* (*c.* 1370), a young woman named May is deceiving her blind and elderly husband, Januarie, by taking a lover called Damyan. The three characters find themselves in a garden, where a pear tree is growing; unbeknown to Januarie, Damyan is hiding in its branches. May expresses a sudden craving for a pear:

> *'Now sire,' quod she, 'for aught that may bityde,*
> *I moste han of the peres that I see,*
> *Or I moot dye, so soore longeth me*
> *To eten of the smale peres grene.'*

Helped by the unwitting Januarie, May climbs into the pear tree where she and Damyan make passionate love. Meanwhile, Januarie unexpectedly finds his sight restored just in time to witness the deceit. The choice of a pear tree for the lovers' meeting had its own sexual connotations, which would have been understood by audiences of the day: in medieval times, the pear's fruit symbolised male genitals. Two centuries after Chaucer, the innuendos were still alive. Shakespeare has Mercutio compare the lovestruck Romeo to a 'poperin pear' in *Romeo and Juliet*, and describes the state of old virginity as being like 'a wither'd pear' in *All's Well that Ends Well*.

John Gerard, in his *Herball* of 1597, describes both the wild pear, which he calls the 'choke pear', and the common or 'tame' pear. 'All Peares,' he says, 'are cold, and all have a binding quality and an earthie substance.' The fruits of wild pear 'may with good successe be laid upon hot swellings in the beginning, as may be the leaves of the tree, which do both binde and coole'. He explains that perry

'… is as wholesome a drinke being taken in small quantity as wine; it comforteth and warmeth the stomacke, and causeth good digestion.' Writing in the seventeenth century, the herbalist Nicholas Culpeper advises that all kinds of pears are useful for binding up wounds, but adds that 'wild pears sooner close up the lips of green wounds than the others'.

There is not a great deal of superstition attached to pear trees in general, although in Ireland it was warned that bringing pear blossom indoors could result in a death in the family. There is, however, an intriguing story surrounding a particular heirloom in East Lothian called the Coalstoun Pear. This is not a tree, as you might imagine, but a single fruit, preserved in a silver box. In the thirteenth century, Hugo de Gifford of Yester, also known as the Wizard of Gifford, bestowed magical properties on the pear, so that it would bring unfailing prosperity to its owner. This enchanted fruit was in the dowry of Marion Hay, daughter of the 2nd Lord Hay of Yester, when she married George Broun, 10th Laird of Coalstoun; it passed safely through successive generations until the late seventeenth century, when the laird's wife, Lady Elizabeth McKenzie, was overcome with curiosity and bit a piece out of it. Misfortune soon followed: the family suffered financial hardship and the estate was sold. A few years later Sir George Broun and both his sons were drowned in the river below the house. The precious fruit is said to have turned rock hard, and still bears the offending teeth marks.

SCOTS PINE

Pinus sylvestris

You may as well forbid the mountain pines
To wag their high tops and to make no noise,
When they are fretten with the gusts of heaven.

WILLIAM SHAKESPEARE, FROM *THE MERCHANT OF VENICE*, ACT IV, SCENE I (C. 1597)

Few trees are more evocative of our prehistoric past than the Scots pine. Tall and majestic, its crusty trunk splashed with delicate hues of pink and orange, and its dark green crown rising high into the clear mountain air, it seems to preserve some essential memory of our ancient forests. The link seems even more tangible when you consider that these trees can live to be 300 years old, and their earliest predecessors arrived in Britain around 10,500 years ago, after the retreat of the last ice sheet; just 35 generations of trees stand between now and then.

The Scots pine is Britain's only native pine. A pioneer species, it reached its maximum extent around 6000BC and was later replaced in many places by oak, birch and other species. Some experts believe that a warm period that encouraged the formation of blanket bog sparked a gradual downturn in the distribution of Scots pine, especially across England and Wales. Its heartland became the 'great wood of Caledon', as the Romans called it, although by the time they arrived it had already dwindled to a fraction of its former size, through human activity combined with climate change. Today, although 99 per cent of the native pinewood has been lost, conservation efforts are bringing about a welcome reversal in its decline.

Although it is one of the most widely distributed species of pine in the world, the Scots pine of the Caledonian pinewoods is of a sub-species of pine unknown outside Scotland. Growing in the company of broadleaved trees, such as birch, rowan and aspen, it creates a rich and diverse habitat for all forms of wildlife, including red squirrel, pine marten, capercaillie and crested tit. It is believed that most of the Scots pines in England and Wales have either been planted, or are self-seeded from planted trees, perhaps many generations ago. An early reference to the planting of Scots pine in England is revealed in a letter from King James I to the Earl of Mar in 1621, requesting pine seedlings for the estate of the Marquis of Rockingham at Burleigh on the Hill.

Scots pines grow straight and tall, some reaching heights of over 100ft (30.5m); this asset, combined with the strength of the timber, helped to hasten the pinewoods' demise from the late seventeenth century onwards. Trunks were favoured for ships' masts and pit props and were even bored and shipped to London for water pipes. Pine was used for waterwheels, railway sleepers, and for all kinds of construction and joinery; the attractive, red-coloured wood was called 'deal', and in Northamptonshire the cones were known as 'deal-apples'. The wood was burned for charcoal to supply iron foundries, and also to produce tar and pitch – substances that were in huge demand for shipbuilding. Tar preserved ships' rigging, and pitch was used to waterproof the hull; sailors would tar their clothes and even their hair! Needless to say, their hands were permanently black: the traditional naval salute, with downward-facing palm, arose from the need to hide tar-stained palms from view.

For centuries, pine beer, which uses pine sprigs instead of hops, was a popular drink in the Highlands, and cottagers burned 'fir candles' – tapers made of pine. In Sir Walter Scott's novel, *Waverley* (1814), the hero of the story is led to the cave of notorious outlaw Donald Bean

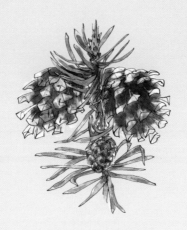

SCOTS PINE
Cones and needles

Lean, where pine torches 'emitted a bright and bickering light, attended by a strong though not unpleasant odour'. Pine resin was apparently chewed by the Vikings; it was known to have antiseptic properties, so it might have helped them with sore throats, but it must have been hard on their teeth. Pine resin is an ingredient in varnishes, wood preservatives and waxes; heating fresh resin produces a hard substance called rosin, used by violinists to improve friction on their bows.

In the late sixteenth century, herbalist John Gerard was reporting that resin mixed in ointments was good for green wounds, and that the tar would heal the 'bitings of Serpents' if combined with salt and applied directly. Steam from boiling fresh pine shoots, which contain aromatic terpenes (a constituent of turpentine) relieved bronchial congestion, while a mouthwash of pine leaves boiled in vinegar was used to ease toothache.

Simply being in the presence of pines can be beneficial: walking through the forest and inhaling the delicious aroma is an invigorating sensation. Pine bath salts are said to offer relief from fatigue, sleeplessness and skin irritations.

> *It is not a theory, but an observation slowly built up that Scotch firs ... are almost certain signs either of the line of an ancient track, or more particularly its sighting points. They are to be seen in twos and threes about the very ancient homesteads, or a thin line of them running along a hill ridge or flank ...*
>
> ALFRED WATKINS, FROM *THE OLD STRAIGHT TRACK* (1925)

To our grandparents and great-grandparents, Scots pines were better known as 'Scotch firs', even though they are not really fir trees. Around the turn of the twentieth century, a Herefordshire man named Alfred Watkins noticed some intriguing features in his local landscape and wrote about them in his book, *The Old Straight Track*. To Watkins, Scots pines, especially on prominent landmarks, were age-old sighting points for travellers. They were certainly used by cattle drovers, right up to the nineteenth century: in *The Drovers' Roads of Wales* (1977), Fay Godwin and Shirley Toulson explain that, for hundreds of years, these herdsmen would follow traditional, well-worn tracks across country as they drove thousands of animals to market. The farms where they could find accommodation and safe pasture were often distinguished by two or three Scots pines.

This tradition was not restricted to Wales: in Yorkshire, 'halfpenny field' was the name for a pine-marked pasture where cattle could be rested. There is also a theory that, after the Jacobite Rebellions in the eighteenth century, a group or avenue of Scots pines planted near an English dwelling signalled a safe haven for fleeing supporters of Bonnie Prince Charlie. More recently, in the nineteenth century Scots pines were planted as hedges known as 'deal rows' in the East Anglian Breckland; now that they are no longer cut, some have grown to maturity and their tall crowns can be seen rising above the heathland.

Some remarkable examples of Scots pines are dotted around the country. On Barnham Cross Common in Norfolk, the Trysting Tree has grown with a looped trunk, and lovers traditionally link hands through the hole. Near New Scone in Perthshire, the 'King of the Forest' has a 20ft (6m) girth and a height of 102ft (31m) – the largest trunk recorded for Scots pine in Britain. A fitting partner is the Queen of the Firs near Aboyne in Aberdeenshire: this majestic lady is 121ft (37m) tall, with a slightly slimmer girth of just over 15ft (4.6m). Some particularly old specimens, dating back perhaps 400 years or more, are growing on the Balmoral Estate. No wonder Queen Victoria, an ardent lover of the Highlands, was enraptured by their beauty.

In Thomas Hardy's *The Woodlanders* (1887), the forester Giles Winterborne and the girl who secretly loves him, Marty South, set out to plant a thousand young pine trees. From living and working in the woodland, Marty's instinctive understanding of trees allows her to sense the life force in their branches: 'She erected one of the young pines into its hole, and held up her finger; the soft musical breathing instantly set in, which was not to cease night or day till the grown tree should be felled – probably long after the two planters should be felled themselves.'

THE FAIRY TREE

ABERFOYLE

On Doon Hill near Aberfoyle in Perthshire, a Scots pine is said to contain the spirit of a seventeenth-century church minister by the name of Robert Kirk. A seventh son, and therefore said to be gifted with second sight, in 1691 Kirk wrote a book called *The Secret Commonwealth of Elves, Faunes and Fairies* which described his encounters with these beings on Doon Hill. They were, he said, 'intelligent studious Spirits … somewhat of the Nature of a condensed Cloud, and best seen in Twilight'.

A year later, Robert Kirk died while walking on his beloved Doon Hill. He was only 48, and the incident was wreathed in mystery. His congregation believed that this was the fairies' revenge for having revealed their secrets; a story grew up that he had been captured and taken away to fairyland, and that his coffin was filled with stones. A Scots pine which grows on top of the cone-shaped hill is said to contain Kirk's spirit, and modern-day visitors hang 'clouties' or strips of cloth on nearby trees in the hope that their wishes will be granted by the fairy folk.

LONDON PLANE

Platanus × hispanica

By far the most common tree in London, representing over half of the city's trees, the London plane is believed to be a fertile hybrid of the Oriental plane (*Platanus orientalis*) and the American plane or buttonwood (*P. occidentalis*). The English botanist John Tradescant had both 'parent' species growing in his Vauxhall garden in 1636, so there is a strong chance that he was the originator.

Other sources state that the hybrid first arose in Spain or southern France in the mid-seventeenth century, but if this is the case, the time and means of its arrival on our shores is still something of a mystery.

In the space of a little under four centuries, however, the London plane has made up for lost time, and this majestic tree is now a much-loved feature of parks and squares, especially in London's West End. Being tolerant of pollution, it is also a popular street tree in many other cities, casting a welcome shade in the heat of summer.

Some of our first London planes were not planted in London at all, but in Cambridgeshire. One specimen, which still stands in the grounds of the Bishop's Palace in Ely, was planted around 1680 by Peter Gunning, Bishop of Ely. Two trees of comparable vintage stand in the grounds of the former Bishop's Palace at Buckden, and were planted by Robert Sanderson, Bishop of Lincoln.

Within Greater London, a magnificent plane tree at Barn Elms, affectionately known as Barney, is believed to be London's oldest and largest, dating back to about 1685. The London planes in Berkeley Square are the oldest living trees in central London, planted in 1789 by Edward Bouverie, son of the 1st Viscount of Folkestone. The tallest of these, the Berkeley Plane, has achieved a height of over 98ft (30m). However, none of these would top the tallest London plane in Britain, and quite possibly in Europe: standing at over 162ft (49.6m), this natural skyscraper is growing with several companions near Bryanston School at Blandford Forum in Dorset.

In the eighteenth century, the London plane was one of the signature trees of landscape designer Lancelot 'Capability' Brown. He ordered dozens of them for his planting scheme at Petworth House in West Sussex, and he may have planted the huge London plane that still stands at the end of the Grecian Valley at Stowe in Buckinghamshire. As Royal Gardener in the reign of George III, Brown included London planes in his design for the pleasure grounds of Buckingham House (now Buckingham Palace).

The London plane's five-lobed leaves are larger than those of sycamore, and the tips are more pointed. In May and June, tiny

male and female flowers appear, grouped together in separate
inflorescences. The female flowers develop into dry fruits known as
achenes, each containing a single seed, and these dangle from the tree
in bristly balls. The bark is a beautiful feature of this tree, forming
scales of brown, cream, grey and green, which are shed regularly to
reveal a smooth patch of trunk or branch; this process is thought to
aid the tree in ridding itself of pollutants.

*The pale-brown wood is fine-grained, tough, and hard, and is extensively
used by pianoforte-makers, coach-builders, and cabinet-makers …*
EDWARD STEP, FROM *WAYSIDE AND WOODLAND TREES* (1904)

Called 'lacewood' in the furniture trade, London plane produces a
beautifully pale and decorative wood, often exhibiting a pattern of
darker flecks and rays. It is used to produce exquisite bowls, small
boxes, and other decorative items.

In *A Tale of Two Cities* (1859), a novel by Charles Dickens set at the
time of the French Revolution, 17-year-old Lucie Manette sits with
her ageing father beneath a plane tree that grows near their lodgings in
London's Soho Square. Dr Manette is still suffering after his years
of incarceration in the Bastille, while Lucie is soon to be married to
Charles Darnay, a French emigré whose family were responsible for
her father's imprisonment. On the eve of Lucie's wedding, she and her
father watch the moon rise through the branches of the plane tree and
afterwards Lucie sees her father safely to bed, hoping that she might be
the true and loving daughter that he deserves: 'So, the sunrise came, and
the shadows of the leaves of the plane-tree moved upon his face, as softly
as her lips had moved in praying for him.'

In the first century AD, it seems that plane trees were a living
first-aid kit. The Roman naturalist Pliny the Elder made the rather
dramatic claim that they neutralised 'the poison of the bat', and went
on to explain that the seed-globules taken in wine would effectively
cure snake bites and scorpion stings. Pounded with vinegar and

LONDON PLANE
Leaves and fruit in autumn

honey, the seeds removed 'freckles, cancerous sores and chronic
pustules on the neck', and the ashes of the burnt globules healed burns
and frostbite. An ointment made from the leaves and bark relieved
gatherings and suppurations, while a decoction of the bark in vinegar
eased sore teeth (*Natural History*, XXIV).

Among the Classical Greek philosophers, plane trees were associated
with poetry, and also with intellectual debate. Perhaps the writer
Sir Arthur Conan Doyle was aware of this latter connection: in 'The
Problem of Thor Bridge' (1922), he mentions that a plane tree
overlooks 221B Baker Street, the home of Sherlock Holmes and his
friend Dr Watson:

> *It was a wild morning in October, and I observed as I was*
> *dressing how the last remaining leaves were being whirled from the*
> *solitary plane tree which graces the yard behind our house.*

BLACK POPLAR

Populus nigra ssp. *betulifolia*

Nor must the Heliad's Fate in Silence pass,
Whose Sorrow first produc'd the Poplar Race;
Their Tears, while at a Brother's Grave they mourn,
To golden Drops of fragrant Amber turn …

RENÉ RAPIN, FROM *OF GARDENS: A LATIN POEM IN FOUR BOOKS*
(1718)

Greek mythology explains how the black poplar came into being. While attempting to drive Apollo's sun-chariot across the sky, Phaethon, the impetuous son of Helios, lost control of the horses, forcing Zeus to strike him down with a thunderbolt. When his seven sisters, known as the Heliades, discovered his death they grieved so much that their limbs began to take root in the ground. The gods pitied them and changed them into black poplar trees, while their tears were preserved as drops of amber.

So-called because its rugged bark can appear black from a distance, black poplar is one of Britain's rarest trees, and it is also one of our most distinctive. Mature specimens can reach a height of 125ft (38m), with a massive trunk that usually leans to one side, and great sweeping branches that have proved ideal for the crucks of buildings. Author and woodland expert Oliver Rackham considers that it is one of the most quintessentially English trees, preserving something of the splendour of our medieval countryside.

Black poplar was not always uncommon in Britain. Many thousands of years ago, it grew in a habitat that has long since disappeared – winter-flooded riverine woods – in the company of ash, alder, birch, elm and willow. To reproduce, male and female trees must grow in proximity with each other, and the fertilised seed must fall on mud which remains damp throughout the summer; but the tree's preferred habitat has been gradually drained and cultivated over the centuries, reducing its population to around 7,000 individuals in Britain, the large majority of which are male. Luckily, the black poplar will sometimes reproduce by putting up suckers from fallen

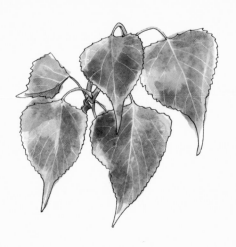

BLACK POPLAR
Leaves

trunks, and even green branches and twigs that fall onto muddy river banks can take root.

Like the aspen, the black poplar's sharply tipped, angular leaves have a habit of rustling in a slight breeze; some folk believed that this sound foretold a coming downpour. It is also known as the water poplar, willow poplar and cotton poplar: the last name comes from the seeds of the female tree, which are coated with cotton-like fluff.

Perhaps Britain's best-known black poplar grew at Aston on Clun in Shropshire. Every year, on 29 May, the villagers decorated it with flags and bunting. This tradition is said to have begun in 1786, to celebrate the wedding of the local squire, John Marston; his wife, Mary Carter, paid for the tree to be dressed every year. The custom may have older roots, however: 29 May is Oak Apple Day, which Charles II declared a public holiday in 1660; and the custom of dressing trees in honour of St Bride or St Bridget goes back much further. The Aston on Clun poplar blew down in 1995, but a cutting has been established on the same site.

The timber of black poplar is fire-resistant, and has been used for floorboards, ships' decking, and in oast houses. Its pale yellowish wood makes attractive bowls and veneers, and because it is light and resists splintering, it was also favoured for shields, clogs and toys. Black poplar lined the floors of carts, and was used for making rifle butts in the Great War. Its branches were lopped to make matches, bean-poles and baskets, and its leaves were fed to cattle in winter.

Public awareness of the black poplar was enhanced in the 1970s by the botanist Edgar Milne-Redhead, who devoted many years of his life to studying its natural history. It occurs in Wales, central Ireland, and in England generally as far north as the Mersey and the Humber, and is a non-woodland tree, preferring meadows and flood plains.

Black poplars appear in several paintings by John Constable, including *The Hay Wain*, and it has been suggested that the hay wain itself – a horse-drawn cart – would have been made of black poplar.

In his *Herball* of 1597, John Gerard advises that 'the leaves and young buds of blacke Poplar asswage the paine of the gout in the hands or feet, being made into an ointment with May butter'. According to seventeenth-century botanist Nicholas Culpeper, 'the water that drops from the hollow places of this tree' will remove warts, weals, and similar 'breakings-out of the body'. He adds that the young buds, bruised in butter, were much used by women to beautify their hair, and that an ointment called 'populeon' was good for drying up the milk in women's breasts when they had weaned their babies.

The timber of black poplar is fire-resistant, and has been used for floorboards, ships' decking, and in oast houses

Writing in the old Dorset dialect, the nineteenth-century poet William Barnes describes how, at the end of a long working day, he would sit at home and watch two big old poplars swaying in the wind. He does not specify if they are *black* poplars, but this is likely because of their apparent size and age. They give him comfort, as they have seen many generations come and go:

> *There yonder poplar trees do plaÿ*
> *Soft music, as their heads do swaÿ,*
> *While wind, a-rustlèn soft or loud,*
> *Do stream ageän their lofty sh'oud;*
> *An' seem to heal the ranklèn zore*
> *My mind do meet wi' out o' door,*
> *When I've a-bore, in downcast mood,*
> *Zome evil where I look'd vor good.*

WILLIAM BARNES, FROM 'THE POPLARS', *POEMS OF RURAL LIFE IN THE DORSET DIALECT,*
SECOND COLLECTION (1863)

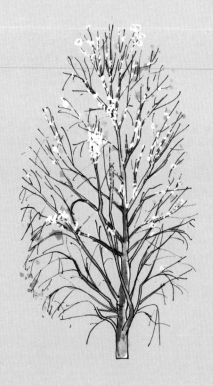

WHITE POPLAR

Populus alba

Accoring to John Evelyn, seventeenth-century connoisseur of all things arboreal, white poplars were beautiful, but best admired from afar: 'The shade of this tree is esteemed very wholesome in Summer but they do not become walks, or avenues by reason of their suckers, and that they foul the ground at fall of the leaf; but they would be planted in barren woods, and to flank places at distance, for their increase, and the glittering brightness of their foliage ...' (*Sylva*, 1664.)

It is certainly true that the white poplar's foliage is bright. It has been described as the whitest tree in the landscape, and from a distance it can appear to be covered with snow – a puzzling illusion on a summer's day. The secret lies in its leaves, which are silvery white on the underside and covered with soft down; even the new shoots have the same pale, velvety coating. On young trees the bark of the trunk is light grey, often pitted with striking diamond-shaped marks; this colour darkens with age. The leaves are lobed, similar to those of field maple. Like the black poplar, it puts forth catkins in spring, with male and female flowers carried on separate trees.

Until recently, it was thought that white poplar was brought to Britain from Holland in the seventeenth century, but the woodland author Oliver Rackham has found reference to it in medieval documents, particularly in Suffolk, under the name of 'abel' or 'abele'. He considers that it is either a native tree or an ancient introduction.

WHITE POPLAR
Leaves

Now widely planted as an ornamental tree, it is likely that its original stronghold would have been the south of England.

The light wood of the white poplar was once favoured by sculptors and woodturners for making into bowls and other decorative items; John Evelyn mentions its use for bellows, ships' pumps, and props for vines and hops, and adds that 'of this material they also made shields of defence in sword and buckler-days'. Chopped and sown in rills with a topping of manure, the bark would produce a good crop of mushrooms.

> *Hercules adorned himself with a crown of poplar, and his worshippers later wore garlands of poplar in his honour*

'The barke ...' says John Gerard, 'is a good remedy for the Sciatica or ache in the huckle [hip] bones, and for the strangury. The same barke is also reported to make a woman barren, if it be drunke with the kidney of a Mule ...' (*The Herball*, 1597.)

In *Plant Lore, Legends and Lyrics*, Richard Folkard (1884) reveals that the white poplar was once considered to be an antidote to the bite of a serpent. In Roman times it was dedicated to the god Hercules, who destroyed the fire-breathing giant Cacus in a cavern on Mount Aventine, which was covered with poplars. To mark his victory, Hercules adorned himself with a crown of poplar, and his worshippers later wore garlands of poplar leaves at ceremonies and sacrifices in his honour. According to Folkard, white poplar was also dedicated to Time, 'because its leaves were constantly in motion, and, being dark on one side and light on the other, they were emblematic of night and day'.

ROWAN

Sorbus aucuparia

The rowan or mountain ash is a tree that relishes a challenge. In the Scottish Highlands, it can often be found growing at altitudes of up to 3,200ft (976m), braving the scouring winds on a bare hillside with its roots firmly lodged inside a rocky crevice. Such specimens are often beautifully gnarled and stunted, like a natural bonsai; in other, more hospitable regions, it can reach a height of around 50ft (15.2m). The rowan is not a typical woodland tree, often preferring a solitary existence on woodland margins, in clearings, or as a wayside tree.

Silvery-grey bark covers the trunk and slender branches, which bear distinctive leaves of around 15 smaller leaflets, arranged in opposing pairs. These have serrated edges, distinguishing them from the leaves of ash trees, which are smooth. In late spring, a froth of creamy blossoms appears, sweet-scented to attract pollinating insects such as bees and beetles.

The number of different folk names for the rowan hint at its long-standing significance among country dwellers. 'Quickbeam', 'wicken', 'witchwood', 'witch-wiggin tree', 'chitchat', 'sip-sap' ... the names suggest affection as well as respect, and in many places there was a strong superstition against cutting one down. 'Rowan ash and red thread / Haud the witches a' in dread', was the old Scottish saying, and a rowan would be planted outside a house to ward off witches, while branches were hung in barns and stables to protect the livestock. The women who drove the cattle up to the summer dwellings or sheilings carried a switch of rowan, and in Strathspey the superstition was carried still further: on the first day of May all the sheep and lambs were driven through a hoop made of rowan branches, an exercise which must have demanded skill and patience.

> *The rowan is not a typical woodland tree, often preferring a solitary existence on woodland margins, in clearings, or as a wayside tree*

On the Isle of Man, where it is known as *cuirn*, rowan twigs were bound into small crosses with sheep's wool and placed over doorways on the eve of May Day, and similar crosses were carried for protection on a sea voyage. Equally important to sailors were the berries, as they are rich in vitamin C and were once consumed to prevent scurvy.

Should an unfortunate person be captured by the fairies and spirited away to their realm, rowan held the key to getting them back. In *Celtic Folklore* (1901), John Rhys explains that it was best to wait until the fairies were dancing in a ring with their captive; two or more strong men should then extend a long stick of mountain ash into the centre of the circle, so that when the human came round to it in his turn, even though he was invisible, he could grasp it and be hauled out. The fairies would not stop him, as they dared not touch the mountain ash.

> *Their spells were vain; the hags return'd*
> *To the queen, in sorrowful mood,*
> *Crying that witches have no power*
> *Where there is roan-tree wood.*
>
> FROM AN OLD NORTHUMBERLAND BALLAD,
> 'THE LAIDLEY WORM OF SPINDLESTON HEUGH' (C. 1270)

In Wales, every old graveyard was said to possess at least one rowan tree, which was believed to protect the souls of those resting within it; in Montgomeryshire, mourners at a funeral would rest the coffin beneath one of these benevolent trees on their way into church.

In *Wayside and Woodland Trees* (1904), Edward Step finds two more interesting names for the rowan – 'Cock-drunks' and 'Hen-drunks' – which he says come from the belief that fowl were intoxicated by eating the berries. Whether or not this is true, in North Wales a drink was certainly made from the fermented fruit: in the early nineteenth century, John MacCulloch reported that 'a liquor is brewed from the berries of the mountain ash ... called *diod griafol*, by only crushing and

ROWAN
Flowers

putting water to them. After standing for a fortnight it is fit for use …
its flavour somewhat resembles perry.'

For centuries, the berries have been gathered and transformed
into sweet and savoury dishes, including jellies to accompany meat
and game. Medicinally, they were taken to alleviate diarrhoea, while
a gargle made from the berries was known to ease a sore throat. In
Ireland, a legend tells of a rowan known as the Quicken Tree of
Dubhros, which had miraculous properties: 'There is in every one
berry of them the exhilaration of wine and the satisfying of old mead,
and whoever shall eat three berries of them, has he completed a hundred
years, he will return to the age of thirty years.' (*Plant Lore, Legends and
Lyrics*, by Richard Folkard, 1884.) The tree was guarded by Searbhan
Lochlannach, a hideous giant; according to the legend, he was slain by
Diarmuid O'Duibhne, whose wife, Grainne, wanted to eat the berries.

In Norse mythology, the rowan held a similar magic. The god Thor was saved from a fast-flowing river when he clung to the branches of a mountain ash. It was believed that rowan was the tree from which the first woman was made, while the first man was fashioned from an ash. Runes were carved on a *run-stafa* or rune-stave made from rowan, and in fact the words 'rune' and 'rowan' are the believed to share the same root.

From late summer onwards the rowan comes into its full glory. Bright scarlet berries hang in heavy clusters from the branches, attracting flocks of fieldfares and redwings, while the leaves glow like embers in hues of fiery red and orange.

The mountain ash
No eye can overlook, when 'mid a grove
Of yet unfaded trees she lifts her head,
Deck'd with autumnal berries, that outshine
Spring's richest blossoms; and ye may have mark'd,
By a brook side or solitary tarn,
How she her station doth adorn; the pool
Glows at her feet, and all the gloomy rocks
Are brighten'd round her.

WILLIAM WORDSWORTH, FROM *THE EXCURSION* (1814)

SPRUCE

Picea spp.

Scientists believe that, some 60,000 years ago, spruce trees may once have grown in the landscape that is now Britain, during a warmer phase of the Devensian period of glaciation.

Norway spruce (*Picea abies*) was reintroduced to Britain in the sixteenth century, while Sitka spruce (*P. sitchensis*), which takes its name from Sitka Island (now Baranof Island) in Alaska, was described

It was Prince Albert who helped to popularise the tradition of bringing a conifer indoors at Christmas

by Archibald Menzies and collected by David Douglas in the early 1800s. Today, both species are widely grown in commercial forestry plantations, and Norway spruce is often cut for Christmas trees.

It was Prince Albert, husband of Queen Victoria, who helped to popularise the tradition of bringing a conifer indoors at Christmas. This was already an old custom in his native Germany, and after a picture was published in *The Illustrated London News*, showing the royal family around a decorated tree, it soon became a much-loved practice in Britain, the glittering decorations perhaps providing an echo of much older celebrations marking the return of the light at the winter solstice. Every Christmas since 1947, the city of Oslo has sent a Norway spruce as a Christmas tree for

SITKA SPRUCE
Cones

London's Trafalgar Square, in thanks for Britain's support of Norway during the Second World War.

Norway spruce provides the 'tonewood' used for building violins, cellos and double bases; it also forms the soundboards of pianos, harps and guitars. Traditionally, the leaves and twigs were crushed to make spruce beer, which was consumed during early sea voyages to prevent scurvy or simply enjoyed as a refreshing drink, as the heroine of Jane Austen's *Emma* (1815) eagerly acknowledged to her friend, Harriet:

> *'I do remember it,' cried Emma; 'I perfectly remember it. Talking about spruce-beer. Oh! Yes – Mr Knightley and I both saying we liked it, and Mr Elton's seeming resolved to learn to like it too.'*

Prized for its strength and comparatively light weight, Sitka spruce wood was used by the Wright brothers in 1903 to build the propeller and frame of the world's first aeroplane, the *Wright Flyer*. During the First World War, spruce timber from America was used to build war planes such as the Airco DH.3, designed by Geoffrey de Havilland, and this method of construction was still being used for some aircraft in the 1940s. The de Havilland Mosquito was built almost entirely of wood, including spruce, birch and ash.

Timber from Sitka spruce plantations is used for construction, paper pulp and biomass chips; the wood is also used to repair vintage aircraft, and to build gliders and model planes.

SYCAMORE

Acer pseudoplatanus

Some historians speculate that the sycamore or 'great maple', a native to Central Europe and Western Asia, may have been brought to Britain by knights returning from the Crusades, while others suggest that wandering monks were the distributors. The folklorist Richard Folkard claims that Scotland's first sycamores were planted by Mary, Queen of Scots in her own garden, possibly because of their religious associations.

With no pollen evidence to track the origins of sycamore – its pollen is identical to that of field maple – we can only describe the sycamore as an archaeophyte, meaning that it was an ancient introduction. Even the name 'sycamore' has a rather confused history, as explained by naturalist Gertrude Clarke Nuttall in *Trees and How They Grow* (1913):

> The true Sycamore is the Ficus Sycomorus, an Eastern tree, whose fruit is like a fig, and whose leaves resemble those of a mulberry ... Tradition always held that Zacchaeus climbed into the Ficus Sycomoros – the true Sycamore – to see Our Lord pass, but in the mystery plays of the Middle Ages, since the true tree did not grow in the West, the Great Maple with its heavy shade was substituted, and hence the Eastern name became attached to it.

The sycamore could therefore claim to have Biblical connections, but these were not enough to impress the seventeenth-century horticulturist John Evelyn, who found the trees intensely annoying: 'The Sycomor ... is much more in reputation for its shade than it deserves; for the Hony-dew leaves, which fall early (like those of the Ash) turn to Mucilage and noxious insects, and putrefie with the first moisture of the season; so as they contaminate and marr our Walks; and are therefore by my consent, to be banish'd from all curious Gardens and Avenues.' (*Sylva*, 1664.)

Despite this dire warning, by the 1800s sycamores had made good their escape from landscaped gardens and begun naturalising themselves, helped no doubt by their tolerance of inhospitable conditions such as windy coastal sites, salt-laden air and industrial pollution.

191

Sycamore leaves are palmate with five distinct lobes, and can grow to over 6in (15cm) in width. The greenish yellow flowers, which appear in spring, hang in small racemes. After pollination by insects, they develop into the familiar winged fruits, known as samaras or 'helicopters' to generations of schoolchildren. Autumn winds send the seeds spiralling down from the tree to land on the woodland floor, where, the following spring, they will lose no time in sending out sturdy shoots to form a forest of saplings.

On mature sycamore trees, the thick flaking bark is curiously patterned and textured, providing thousands of little crevices for insects to hide in. A fine example of this is the Birnam Sycamore, a massive, 300-year-old retainer which stands in solemn dignity just a stone's throw from the more famous Birnam Oak at Dunkeld in Perthshire. Its long, mossy limbs and beautifully patterned bark are impressive in their own right, and its crown seems to extend right up into the sky.

A sprig of sycamore was said to prevent mischievous fairies from spoiling the milk

To some people, including many conservationists, the sycamore is seen an invasive tree, stealing light from the seedlings of other species with its dense canopy of leaves, and supporting comparatively little wildlife. However, it hosts high numbers of aphids, an important food source for birds; these aphids are responsible for the sticky secretion of 'honeydew' that so irritated John Evelyn and still drips from street trees onto unwarily parked cars. Sycamore flowers are a source of pollen for bees, while the seeds are eaten by birds and small mammals, and caterpillars of several moth species munch on the leaves.

Traditionally, sycamore sap has been used to make ale, and in Montgomeryshire a sprig of sycamore was said to prevent mischievous fairies from spoiling the milk. The pale cream wood has a fine

SYCAMORE
Leaves and flowers

grain, making it ideal for furniture and veneer, kitchenware, musical instruments and ornaments. Sycamore was fashioned into clogs and is still chosen for making Welsh love spoons, which are traditionally carved out of a single piece of wood.

In parts of the West Country, sycamore leaves were gathered and used as the base on which to bake small cakes at Easter or harvest time; when they came out of the oven, the cakes had a distinctive leaf pattern on the underside. On Helm Common near Kendal, children would walk beneath the branches of a sycamore known as the Wishing Tree. After making a wish, they would pick up a stone from the path, spit on it, and place it on a nearby drystone wall. Another game was to make miniature waterwheels by impaling four single samaras onto a blackthorn spike and balancing them on two Y-shaped twigs over a stream.

Over the centuries, sycamores have lent themselves very well to the purpose of hanging-trees, as their lower limbs grow thick, long and straight. Examples still stand in the grounds of Leith Hall,

Aberdeenshire, and Blairquhan Castle, Ayrshire. Some sycamores were also known as 'dule' or 'dool' trees, from the Gaelic *deurshuil*, meaning 'weeping eye': these were remembrance trees, where a chieftain and his followers would stand to mourn the loss of their kinsmen.

A strange story is attached to a sycamore in Finnis, County Down. Early in the twentieth century it was believed that the area around the bridge in the village was haunted; a local priest succeeded in capturing the evil spirit in a bottle, which he secreted, for reasons known only to himself, inside the trunk of a sycamore tree. Although the hauntings ceased, the tree itself became the object of fear and superstition, and subsequently died. Only the gaunt trunk and a couple of withered limbs remained, but when new power lines were being routed through the village, the workmen were asked to run the cables through the tree instead of cutting it down.

On the wild and windswept moorland around Haworth, West Yorkshire, two twisted sycamores stand next to a ruined farmhouse which is said to have given Emily Brontë the inspiration for *Wuthering Heights* (1847). In the novel, when Mr Earnshaw arrives home from Liverpool with the young Heathcliff, he is disappointed to find that the fiddle he has brought with him as a present for his son has been crushed into pieces. In 2018, a special violin was made to celebrate the 200th anniversary of the author's birth, using sycamore wood from a tree which grew close to the family home.

> *To dream of the Sycamore-tree portends jealousy to the married;*
> *but to the virgin it prognosticates a speedy marriage.*
> RICHARD FOLKARD, FROM *PLANT LORE, LEGENDS AND LYRICS* (1884)

While the sycamore is not widely used in traditional remedies, its presence certainly had a beneficial effect on William Wordsworth, when he re-visited the Wye Valley in 1798.

Five years have past; five summers, with the length
Of five long winters! and again I hear
These waters, rolling from their mountain-springs
With a soft inland murmur. – Once again
Do I behold these steep and lofty cliffs,
That on a wild secluded scene impress
Thoughts of more deep seclusion; and connect
The landscape with the quiet of the sky.
The day is come when I again repose
Here, under this dark sycamore, and view
These plots of cottage-ground, these orchard-tufts,
Which at this season, with their unripe fruits,
Are clad in one green hue, and lose themselves
'Mid groves and copses …

FROM 'LINES COMPOSED A FEW MILES ABOVE TINTERN ABBEY'

THE CORSTORPHINE
SYCAMORE

EDINBURGH

According to tradition, a large sycamore that stood in the heart of Corstorphine on the outskirts of Edinburgh was planted by a monk in the fifteenth century. In 1679, it was a silent witness to the murder of Lord Forrester, a local landowner. A notorious womaniser, Forrester had seduced his niece, Lady Christian Nimmo. Lady Christian waited for him to leave the tavern one night, and in the heat of a quarrel she drew his sword from its scabbard and stabbed him. She fled the scene but was later caught and executed in Edinburgh.

The Corstorphine Sycamore soon developed the reputation of being haunted by a white lady, and local schoolchildren would dare each other to play beneath its branches. It was said that Forrester had buried some treasure beneath the tree, and that every spring this treasure gave a golden hue to the fresh leaves. Unable to resist, one night a villager decided to have a dig around, but was commanded by an eerie voice to stop at once.

In 1998, a storm snapped the tree in two. Residents were saddened by the loss, and local carpenters were commissioned to create something of lasting beauty from the timber. Clocks, boxes, vases, chalices and even violins were fashioned lovingly from the fallen wood, so that the memory of the Corstorphine Sycamore is preserved. In recent years, new shoots have pushed up from the stump, proving that there is still life in this formidable old tree.

THE TOLPUDDLE
MARTYRS' TREE

DORSET

An old sycamore tree in the village of Tolpuddle in Dorset preserves the memory of six men, all of them agricultural labourers, who dared to protest against decreasing wages. In 1834, George Loveless, his brother James, along with James Brine, James Hammett, and father and son Thomas and John Stanfield, formed the Friendly Society of Agricultural Labourers. They held meetings under the tree, agreeing that they would refuse to work for less than 10 shillings per week. Their society was, in effect, an early trade union; while this in itself was not illegal, a local magistrate had them tried under the Unlawful Oaths Act. When they were found guilty, they were sent to penal colonies in Australia. George Loveless is said to have taken with him a leaf from the sycamore tree, pressed between the pages of his Bible.

With the mens' families struggling to survive, a public outcry ensued. The cause gained widespread support, and 100,000 protesters took part in a march through London. As a result, all the workers were pardoned on condition of good conduct, and brought home. Some decided to remain in England, while others moved to Canada. The Martyrs' Tree is a living memory of the men who stood firm in friendship and self-belief.

WALNUT

Juglans regia

It is most likely that the Romans introduced the common walnut into Britain. In their time, it was already a well-known and respected tree: as legend had it, the gods fed upon walnuts, whose Latin name, *Jovis glans*, meant 'the nuts of Jupiter'. This name later contracted into *Juglans*, with the addition of *regia*, meaning 'royal'. The tree's common name comes from the Old English *wealhhnutu*, meaning 'foreign nut' – a reminder of its newness to well-established inhabitants who must have been much more familiar with the hazelnut.

Throughout Europe, the walnut was widely cultivated both for its nuts and for its highly prized and beautiful wood. John Evelyn's *Sylva* (1664) gives one example of its importance: 'In several places betwixt Hanaw and Frankfort in Germany no young farmer whatsoever is permitted to marry a wife, till he bring proof that he hath planted, and is a father of such a stated number of Walnut-trees; and the law is inviolably observed to this day, for the extraordinary benefit which this tree affords the inhabitants.'

Although the walnut has been in Britain for the best part of 2,000 years, it has not become widely naturalised, unlike other species such as the sycamore which arrived later and sallied forth into new territory with no hesitation at all. There was a time when many cottage gardens were planted with at least one walnut tree, and they were popular in country parks, where they could grow into magnificent specimens; some of these still survive, and are a majestic sight with heavy, twisting branches and a wide crown that can rise to 100ft (30.5m).

The walnut's homeland is a vast region that extends from south-eastern Europe through the Himalayas to south-west China. In Britain it demands long, hot summers for its nuts to ripen properly. The leaves have between five and nine paired oval leaflets, with one terminal leaflet at the end; they emit a strong smell, which has been likened to shoe polish! Walnut trees could arguably be described as quite antisocial: the leaves contain a compound called juglone, which

201

is toxic to nearby plants, meaning that very little vegetation can grow around the tree. Insects are also repelled, and it is thought that horses were often tethered beneath them to keep biting flies at bay. This may explain why many English coaching inns are named The Walnut Tree.

Male and female flowers are borne on the same tree, before the leaves appear; the male flowers take the form of green catkins, while the female flowers are spherical, with feathery stigmas protruding from the top. The fleshy fruits may be harvested and pickled while still green or left until the nut inside matures. Walnut trees were traditionally pruned on St Swithin's Day (15 July), and as the nuts were ripening the trees were thrashed or 'brushed' with poles, a practice which was believed to improve the crop. This gave rise to an offensive saying which is repeated – largely apologetically – by several writers of the sixteenth and seventeenth centuries: 'A dog and a wife and a walnut-tree, the more they are beaten the better they be.'

While offering tasty and nutritious eating, walnuts were thought to have other properties that must have been prized for centuries and made it more than worthwhile for the pickers to stain their hands with the dark brown juice that issues from the leaves and fruit. John Gerard noted that the dried nuts, eaten with a fig and a little rue, would 'withstand poyson, prevent and preserve the body from the infection of the plague, and being plentifully eaten they drive wormes forth of the belly'. Walnut oil smoothed and softened the face and hands, and milk made from the kernels 'cooleth and pleaseth the appetite of the languishing sicke body'. Should you have the misfortune to be bitten by a mad dog or a mad man, a mixture of walnuts, onions, salt and honey was highly effective if applied to the wound. On the whole, it sounds as if walnuts were an essential item in the medieval larder.

The greene and tender Nuts boyled in Sugar and eaten as Suckad, are a most pleasant and delectable meat, comfort the stomacke and expell poison.
JOHN GERARD, FROM *THE HERBALL* (1597)

Pliny the Elder, writing in the first century AD, recommended that walnut shells, burnt and beaten with oil or wine, would promote the growth of hair when applied to a baby's head; he added that the same treatment could be used for mange. Very old walnuts were a cure for gangrene, carbuncles and bruises, while a walnut shell placed in a hollow tooth would cauterise it.

A mature walnut tree can produce between two and three thousand nuts, but by that age it is also coveted for its wood. The beautiful figuring of polished burr walnut was, and still is, prized for furniture, veneers, and all kinds of decorative items. The best wood is found in the root crown, so instead of felling the trees in the normal manner, they were cut down about 3ft (0.9m) above ground and the remaining stump was dug up, complete with the root ball.

One of the traditional uses of walnut is for gun stocks, because it can hold the fine screws that are used to fix wood to metal, and it is able to withstand the impact of firing. During the Peninsular War in the early 1800s, when Britain, Spain and Portugal pitted themselves

WALNUT
Walnuts

against the might of Napoleon's empire, so great was the demand for gun stocks that a single walnut tree was worth £600 (equivalent to over £49,000 today). During this time, and in the decades that followed, many of Britain's walnut trees fell to the saw.

As far as superstitions go, it was believed that walnut trees were never struck by lightning, and that a falling walnut tree was an omen of ill fortune. The armies of the Duke of Wellington were obviously not swayed by fanciful prophecies, or else the principle did not apply to manual felling! John Evelyn noted that travellers may be 'both refreshed with the fruit and the shade' of walnut trees, which he greatly admired. He added, however, that in Italy, where sleeping under trees was enjoyed, the shade of a walnut was believed to be particularly unwholesome. The fragrance of shoe polish might have had something to do with that.

> *It was believed that walnut trees were never struck by lightning, and that a falling walnut tree was an omen of ill fortune*

Perhaps Jane Austen, in *Sense and Sensibility* (1811), suspected that some misfortune was attached to the felling of walnut trees – or at least, she used it to convey a sense of wanton destruction. When Elinor Dashwood meets her step-brother, John, in London, she hears about the changes that he is bringing to Norland Park, her beloved former home:

> 'There is not a stone laid of Fanny's green-house, and nothing but the plan of the flower-garden marked out.'
> 'Where is the green-house to be?'
> 'Upon the knoll behind the house. The old walnut trees are all come down to make room for it …'

Dismayed at the news, Elinor 'kept her concern and her censure to herself ...'

Despite the loss of many of our walnut trees, there are still some productive orchards in the south of England. A grove of about 30 trees can be found in Suffolk; the nuts, which are harvested between September and November, have occasionally graced the royal table.

Another species of walnut, the black walnut (*J. nigra*), is also present in the UK, having been introduced from the North America; *The New Sylva* (2014) by Gabriel Hemery and Sarah Simblet notes that the first record of a growing tree was in 1656, and John Evelyn was enthusiastic about its potential. Black walnut can reach even greater heights than the common walnut and produces nuts with a very thick husk.

WAYFARING TREE
AND GUELDER ROSE

Viburnum lantana and *Viburnum opulus*

*The Viburnum, or Way-faring-tree, growing plentifully in every corner,
makes pins for the yokes of oxen; and superstitious people think that it protects
their cattle from being bewitched and plant the shrub about their stalls.*

JOHN EVELYN, FROM *SYLVA* (1664)

Inhabiting the sunny woodland edges and hedgerows of southern England and Wales, the wayfaring tree sports umbels of fragrant creamy-white flowers in spring. A few months later, these are transformed into clusters of berries that turn from green to red and then black, providing a feast for thrushes and warblers; meanwhile the leaves put on a rich autumn display of orange and gold.

The wood of the wayfaring tree is hard and densely grained and has been used for the wooden pins holding the yokes of oxen – partly for superstitious reasons, as it was believed to protect the cattle. 'Coven-tree', one of its many local names, suggests a whiff of witchcraft. It is also good for arrow shafts: Ötzi, the Neolithic man whose body was recovered from an Austrian glacier in 1991, was carrying arrows made of viburnum wood.

Young branches were used for binding sheaves and bundles, and for twisting into whip handles, giving rise to another name, 'twistwood'. In Wiltshire, it is known as 'hoar withy', referring to its hairy leaves and buds and its willow-like flexibility – 'withy' being an old word for willow. Other names include 'whipcrop' and 'lithe-worth', while 'cotton-tree', 'mealy-tree' and 'white-wood' arise from the dusty appearance of its young shoots and leaves.

In old herbal remedies, the leaves and berries were used to make a gargle and settle the stomach

In old herbal remedies, the leaves and berries were used to make a gargle and settle the stomach; writing in the seventeenth century, John Evelyn noted that the crushed leaves 'not only colour the hairs black, but fasten their roots'. The bark of the tree's root, boiled and beaten, served as bird lime, which was smeared on branches to trap birds.

How did the wayfaring tree get its name? Gertrude Clarke Nuttall claims that it was so-called by the sixteenth-century botanist John Gerard, because it was 'ever on the road'. Some naturalists have questioned the justification of this, since many other trees can be found

WAYFARING TREE
Flower

on paths and tracks, but Nuttall finds a delightful answer: it is, she explains, the tree itself that is wayfaring, not the possible passer-by.

Haunting woodland clearings and old hedgerows, the guelder rose occurs throughout Britain, although it is scarce in Scotland. Its three-lobed leaves turn vivid scarlet in autumn, and these are accompanied by clusters of brilliant red berries which have inspired its colloquial names of 'cranberry tree' and 'dog rowan tree'. Because it likes damp places, it is also known as 'water elder'.

> *For any one who enjoys the sight of red berries in the most jewel-like splendour there is nothing in winter like the viburnum ... if you meet with a fine specimen just when it is caught by the level rays of a crimson sunset, you will behold a shrub that seems to have come from that garden of Aladdin where the fruits of the trees were jewels.*
> PHILIP GILBERT HAMERTON, FROM *THE SYLVAN YEAR* (1882)

According to Edward Step, the name guelder rose 'is a strange case of transference from a cultivated to a wild plant: the variant *sterilis* … was first cultivated in Gelderland; so [John] Gerard tells us that "it is called in Dutch, Gheldersche Roose; in English, Gelder's Rose."' (*Wayside and Woodland Trees*, 1904.)

In the Cotswolds, the tree was known as King's Crown, because the King of the May was traditionally crowned with a wreath of it. The berries contain a powerful anti-spasmodic which is still used by some herbalists to treat asthma and menstrual cramp.

WHITEBEAM

Sorbus aria

Whitebeams are perhaps best admired in spring, when their leaves are just emerging from the bud. Pale and silvery, covered with soft down, they stand upright like little tongues of flame, revealing the delicate veining on their undersides. Later, when they have fully opened, the leaves are seen to be oval and irregularly toothed; the upper surface turns a richer green over time, while the underside retains its coat of silver down.

Sweetly scented, creamy-white flowers ripen into round, bright red fruits, larger than those of the hawthorn or mountain ash. Popular with birds, squirrels and hedgehogs, for many centuries they have also been enjoyed as a seasonal treat by humans, although they are bitter when first picked and must be kept until they 'blet' or start to decay. In Lancashire and Cumbria they are known as 'chess-apples', while in south-west England the larger, brownish fruits of the Devon whitebeam (also known as French hales) were traditionally sold in local markets.

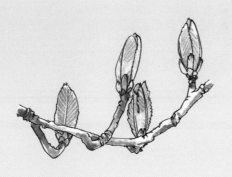

WHITEBEAM
New leaves in spring

Forming a narrow dome that can reach a height of 75ft (23m), the common whitebeam has a beautiful presence in woodlands across southern England. A native tree, it occurs naturally as far north as Derbyshire and has been widely planted elsewhere. Other varieties exist: in *The New Sylva* (2014), Gabriel Hemery and Sarah Simblet note that over 40 taxa within the *Sorbus* genus comprise about half of Britain's native trees. Most, however, are very rare. The Arran whitebeam grows on the Isle of Arran, while the cliff whitebeam has the spirit of a rock climber, clinging on to wind-scoured hillsides high in the Cairngorms. New species are still being identified: 76 specimens of White's whitebeam were discovered in 2005, growing in the Avon Gorge in Bristol, and in 2014 the *New Journal of Botany* described six more new species that have been found around the River Severn and its estuary.

> *The cliff whitebeam has the spirit of a rock climber, clinging on to wind-scoured hillsides high in the Cairngorms*

Old country names for the whitebeam include 'hen-apple', 'whittenbeam', 'white-rice', 'hoar withy' and 'quickbeam', although the last has also been given to the mountain ash. In Lancashire they were known as 'sea owlers', possibly from the alder, whose leaves are quite similar.

Evenly grained and hardwearing, the pale wood is prized by woodturners and joiners, and it has been used for gunstocks and cog-wheels. Few remedies or traditions are associated with it, although in Ireland the whitebeam is said to be a symbol of royal authority.

WILD SERVICE TREE

Sorbus torminalis

Many pubs in Kent, Sussex and Surrey called The Chequers may well owe their name to wild service trees that were growing nearby at some stage in their history. The species was also known as the chequer-tree, possibly because of the speckled pattern on its fruits, the juice of which was added to beer and spirits to enhance the flavour. Until fairly recent times, the inn sign at The Chequers Inn in Smarden, Kent, was decorated with garlands of wild service berries every autumn.

Picked while still under-ripe, the small pear-shaped brown fruits also held a strong appeal for children, who would thread them on strings and hang them up in their homes to ripen. When they started to 'blet' or decompose, by which time they had lost their bitterness, they were eaten like sweets: the flesh has hints of apricot, tamarind and sultana. In the nineteenth century, all the local children knew where the wild service trees grew in Epping Forest in Essex, even though they were scarce, and every autumn they went enthusiastically in search of the fruit, which they called 'sarves', 'sarvers' or 'sarvies'.

> *Though nuts have long been glean'd by many crews*
> *Of shatter'd poor, who daily rambled there;*
> *And squirrels claim'd the remnant as their dues;*
> *Still to the woods the hungry boys repair;*
> *Brushing the long dead grass with anxious feet,*
> *While round their heads the stirr'd boughs patter down*
> *To seek the bramble's jet-fruit, lushy sweet, –*
> *Or climbing service-berries ripe and brown.*

JOHN CLARE, FROM 'THE LAST OF AUTUMN', *THE SHEPHERD'S CALENDAR* (1827)

After the last glacial period, wild service tree may have been one of the later arrivals to Britain; today it is found in scattered populations across much of lowland England as far north as the Lake District. It is present in Wales, but only in localised pockets. Its stronghold seems to be the southern and eastern counties of England: John

WILD SERVICE TREE
Fruit

Gerard observed that 'in Kent it groweth in great aboundance, especially about Southfleet and Gravesend'. (*The Herball*, 1597.) In the Cotswolds, its local name 'lizzory' or 'lezzory' is thought to derive from 'alizier', one of the French words for the tree, while in the Wyre Forest the trees that still grow along the Dowles Brook are quite possibly the legacy of mill-owners who encouraged their growth in former centuries, as the wood was ideal for making cogs for mill machinery.

'Service tree' is an intriguing name and is thought by some to derive from *cerevisia*, a Latin word for beer; alternatively, it may have evolved from *Sorbus*, while another source quotes the Old English word *syfre*. Wild service tree was a common feature in the Northamptonshire landscape, and the poet John Clare called it by its local name of 'surrey'. In the Rockingham Forest area, the branches were used for the beating of the parish boundaries, and they were also carried at the head of village processions.

In addition to cog-making, the pale wood was highly prized for furniture and cabinet work, axles and cart wheels, billiard cues and the screws for wine presses, and for the shafts of arrows; it was the preferred wood for harpsichord jacks, and was coppiced for hop poles in the south of England. In 1260, there is a record that two wild service trees were cut from Havering Park in Essex and taken to the Tower of London, in order to make crossbows for the court of King Henry III.

It is possible that wild service wood was also used for building; in the Weald of Kent and Sussex in particular, mature trees can reach over 16ft (5m) in circumference and yield substantial planks and beams which hold their shape without splitting or shrinking. Many instances of its use in houses may have gone unrecorded, but in the seventeenth century John Evelyn wrote of a room in Surrey which was 'curiously wainscotted' in wild service wood. The logs made good firewood and charcoal, and Epping Forest contains many old pollarded trees that were used for this purpose. This widespread practice goes back a long way, because among the archaeological finds at the Iron Age fort of Maiden Castle in Dorset, charcoal made from wild service wood has been identified.

At the Iron Age fort of Maiden Castle, charcoal made from wild service wood has been identified

If left untouched, wild service can achieve a height of over 80ft (24.4m), with a profusion of bright green leaves that may, at first glance, be mistaken for maple. The small, faintly scented white flowers are pollinated by insects, but in Britain they produce very little seed, possibly because the tree is on the limit of its northern range and ideally prefers warmer temperatures. In autumn, the leaves turn vivid shades of orange, gold and red.

As well as being good to eat, the berries were gathered for their medicinal properties: the tree's Latin species name *torminalis* comes

216

from *tormina*, meaning 'gripe'. John Gerard advises that the fruits 'stay all maner of fluxes in the belly, the bloudy flix and vomiting', and notes their additional use for stanching bleeding 'if they be cut and dried in the sun before they be ripe, and so reserved for use'. (*The Herball*, 1597.)

In his *Sylva* (1664), John Evelyn says that water distilled from the flower stalks and leaves 'is incomparable for consumptive and tabid [wasting] bodies ...' and claims that 'distilled warm into the ears, it abates the pain', presumably of ear-ache. He claims that it cures a mysterious complaint which he describes as 'the green-sickness in virgins', and reports that the salt of the wood, taken in decoction of *althaea* (mallow), is an excellent remedy 'to break and expel gravel [kidney stones]'.

WILLOWS, SALLOWS AND OSIERS

Salix spp.

Britain hosts at least 18 native species of willow, and since they hybridise freely, identification can be something of a puzzle, even for experienced botanists. They are distributed across a wide range of habitats, from the banks of lazily meandering rivers where old pollarded willows bend to admire their reflections in the water, to the windswept heights of over 4,000ft (1,220m) in the Cairngorms, a bleak and unforgiving environment of winter blizzards and sub-zero temperatures.

It is believed that willows were among the first trees to recolonise the British landscape after the last glacial period, in the company of juniper and birch. Both male and female trees bear catkins, and the tiny seeds, coated in soft, silky hairs, are later dispersed by the wind. The leaves vary in shape, from the long tapering fingers of white willow (*Salix alba*) to the more oval-shaped, finely felted leaves of the sallows, including common sallow (*S. cinerea*). As for height, there is even more contrast, as the white willow is capable of topping 100ft (30.5m), while in the mountain screes, downy willow (*S. lapponum*) and woolly willow (*S. lanata*) hug the ground with short branches.

One of the best-loved willows is surely goat willow, commonly known as 'pussy willow' for its endearing, kitten-soft catkins which emerge from the bud in spring, braving the winter blast while other trees, except for the hazel, are still largely dormant. In his poem 'The Palm Willow' (*The Shorter Poems of Robert Bridges*, 1890), Robert Bridges describes a spring snowstorm whitening the fields and silencing the joyful birdsong:

> The woodland willow stands a lonely bush
> Of nebulous gold;
> There the Spring-goddess cowers in faint attire
> Of frightened fire.

In Cheshire, sprigs of pussy willow were traditionally brought into church on Palm Sunday; but across the border in Shropshire, where they were known as 'goosy goslins' or 'geese and gullies', there was a strong superstition against bringing them indoors, in case no real-life goslings were hatched! Herefordshire folk allowed pussy willow indoors on May Day, when it was thought to be lucky, and a sprig was believed to guard against ill fortune if given by a friend. In Ireland, wayfarers took a 'sally rod' with them for protection on a long journey.

> *A sprig was believed to guard against ill fortune if given by a friend*

Since the very earliest times of human settlement in Britain, willows have been important in everyday life, finding a vast range of uses. The lightweight timber is easy to work, making good tool handles and thatching spars, while the pliant branches of osiers were woven into baskets, cradles and screens and used for tying hurdles. In the Somerset Levels, where ancient man-made trackways cross the marshes, willow is still pollarded and harvested in a tradition that stretches back to the Neolithic period.

The word 'willow' comes from the Anglo-Saxon *welig*, suggesting pliancy and willingness; willows and osiers that were used for weaving were called 'withy trees' or 'withies'. Withycombe in Devon means 'valley of the withies' while the Cornish word for willow is *heligen*. *Saugh-trees* in the Scots dialect meant 'sallows', as described in Allan Ramsay's 1725 pastoral comedy *The Gentle Shepherd*:

> *To where the saugh-tree shades the mennin-pool,*
> *I'll frae the hill come down, when day grows cool …*
> (A MENNIN-POOL IS A MINNOW POOL.)

Willow bark and leaves have valuable remedial properties, as they contain salicylic acid, which is the main component of modern-day aspirin. Chewing willow twigs for the relief of headaches is a centuries-old practice, while infusions were made of the bark and

GOAT WILLOW
'Pussy willow' in spring

leaves to produce a natural painkiller that would relieve gout, earache, toothache and many other aches and pains.

Even the feathery down that coats the catkins found a useful purpose, being collected as a soft stuffing for mattresses, while the dried foliage was valuable as winter fodder for cattle. In Ireland and Wales, willow laths formed the framework of small boats known as coracles, and the traditional Irish harp was fashioned from willow.

With its high resistance to impact and its natural spring, willow wood is a traditional choice for cricket bats, and in some places the trees are grown specifically for this purpose. The wood, which should ideally have a straight grain, is harvested when the tree is around 15–20 years old, and cut into lengths or 'clefts' which are air-dried for a year before shaping into finished bats.

Outside the isle a shallow boat
Beneath a willow lay afloat,
Below the carven stern she wrote,
'The Lady of Shalott' …

In Alfred, Lord Tennyson's poem published in 1833, the boat carrying the doomed Lady of Shalott drifts downriver past 'willowy hills and fields'. Throughout folklore and literature, willow is a symbol of grief and forsaken love: Virgil's *Aeneid* (*c.* 19BC) tells how Dido, Queen of Carthage, stood with a sprig of willow in her hand, mourning her departed lover, Aeneas. The Victorian folklorist Thomas Thiselton-Dyer explains that '… it was customary for those who were forsaken in love to wear a garland made of willow.' (*The Folk-lore of Plants,* 1889.) Rejected lovers are still said to be 'wearing the willow'.

Thou art to all lost love the best,
The only true plant found,
Wherewith young men and maids distrest,
And left of love, are crown'd.

When once the lover's rose is dead,
Or laid aside forlorn:
Then willow-garlands 'bout the head
Bedew'd with tears are worn.

When with neglect, the lovers' bane,
Poor maids rewarded be
For their love lost, their only gain
Is but a wreath from thee.

And underneath thy cooling shade,
When weary of the light,
The love-spent youth and love-sick maid
Come to weep out the night.

ROBERT HERRICK, 'TO THE WILLOW-TREE' (1648)

This association with sorrow may go back to the Biblical story of the exiled Israelites by the waters of Babylon, who wept and hung their harps in willow trees (although the trees in question are now considered to be poplars). The Latin name of the weeping willow (*S. babylonica*), introduced to Britain from northern China, seems to reflect this story; the tree's beautifully pendulous branches, with leaves languidly kissing the water, are now a familiar sight on river banks and in parks and gardens.

Even the gnats in John Keats's 'To Autumn' (1819) seem to have caught a sense of melancholy, either from the willow trees or from the season's fading warmth:

Then in a wailful choir the small gnats mourn
Among the river sallows, borne aloft
Or sinking as the light wind lives or dies;
And full-grown lambs loud bleat from hilly bourn;
Hedge-crickets sing; and now with treble soft
The red-breast whistles from a garden-croft;
And gathering swallows twitter in the skies.

YEW

Taxus baccata

Gall of goat, and slips of yew
Sliver'd in the moon's eclipse ...
WILLIAM SHAKESPEARE, FROM *MACBETH*, ACT IV, SCENE I (C. 1606)

In Shakespeare's notoriously dark 'Scottish play', why was the yew chosen as one of the ingredients that were thrown into the witches' cauldron? Not only that, why did it have to be cut during an eclipse of the moon?

The most obvious answer is that all parts of the yew, except for the fleshy parts of its fruits, are toxic. Cattle and deer can browse on the leaves in small quantities without too much ill effect, eventually developing an immunity, but the fact remains that yew has been known to be poisonous since early times and may even have given rise to the word 'toxic'. The naturalist Edward Step explains:

> *The tree was named Taxus in Latin, from the Greek toxon*
> *(a bow), because of the ancient repute of its wood for making*
> *that instrument. The tree was held to be poisonous, and so its*
> *name in the form of toxicum came to designate all poisons.*
> FROM *WAYSIDE AND WOODLAND TREES* (1904)

In view of its fearsome reputation, yew would therefore have been a serious omission from the cauldron stirred by Shakespeare's witches, and with its widespread distribution throughout Britain, it was also one of the easiest ingredients to locate, even on a stormy Scottish hillside during a lunar eclipse. Presumably this last requisite made its dark powers even darker.

Edward Step refers to the demand for yew wood in bow-making, and it was indeed chosen for longbows, as well as for spears and dagger handles. Neolithic longbows made of yew have been dug up from the peat in Somerset and the Scottish Borders, and the world's oldest known wooden implement is a yew spear, believed to be around 420,000 years old, which was discovered in 1911 on the foreshore at Clacton in Essex.

Before the Battle of Bannockburn in 1314, Robert the Bruce is said to have ordered wood from yews growing at Ardchattan Priory on Loch Etive, in order to make longbows. Writing in his *Arboretum et Fruticetum Britannicum* (1838), J. C. Loudon reveals that 'in 1397, Richard II, holding a parliament in a temporary building, on account of the wretched state of Westminster Hall, surrounded his hut with 4,000 Cheshire archers, armed with tough yew bows, to insure the freedom of debate.' It seems that this ancient tradition even gave rise to the word 'yeoman':

> *It signified, originally, a Yewman, so called from bearing the bow in battle, bows being made of yew. Hence, a Yeoman was, at first, of at least equal consequence with an Esquire, or shield-bearer; and, as a proof of this, we have even now Yeomen of the crown, Yeomen of the guards, Yeomen of the chamber &c. – all persons of the first rank.*
> THE MIRROR OF LITERATURE, AMUSEMENT AND INSTRUCTION, VOL. 1 (1821)

Yew wood was such a precious commodity that at one time its export from Britain was banned, and whole plantations were created specifically for bow-wood. The *Mary Rose*, Henry VIII's famous warship, carried several yew bows measuring 6½ft (2m) long. These would have had a draw length of nearly 30in (76cm) and a draw weight of up to 185lb (84kg), posing a serious challenge for most modern archers.

> *Beneath those rugged elms, that yew-tree's shade,*
> *Where heaves the turf in many a mould'ring heap,*
> *Each in his narrow cell for ever laid,*
> *The rude forefathers of the hamlet sleep.*
> THOMAS GRAY, FROM 'ELEGY WRITTEN IN A COUNTRY CHURCHYARD' (1751)

The yew is among the world's longest-lived trees, and some examples are thousands of years old; even when it appears to be dying, an ancient yew can still generate fresh life, because new trees will take root where its branches touch the ground. Today, the British Isles are home to most of the world's ancient yews, and of these, over 80 per cent can be found in churchyards. One explanation is that they were planted there for protection from browsing animals, since farmers would not allow their animals onto consecrated ground.

There may be a much deeper and older reason for the yew's fondness for graveyards, however. Long before the arrival of Christianity, the yew had a profound significance in our culture, being associated with immortality and rebirth. In Irish mythology the yew was known as the Tree of Ross, 'the offspring of the tree that is in Paradise', and legendary battles were fought over its ownership. Druids carried divining rods made of yew and used its wood to kindle ceremonial fires.

> *Long before the arrival of Christianity, the yew had a profound significance, being associated with immortality and rebirth*

With the advent of Christianity, the old beliefs connected to yew were absorbed and adapted by the church. Some historians have speculated that yews were planted to mark a hermit's cell, as described in a medieval Irish poem:

> *There is here above the brotherhood*
> *A bright tall glossy yew;*
> *The melodious bell sends out a*
> *clear keen note*
> *In Saint Columba's church …*

Often, old yew trees can be found growing on blind springs or wells that have since been incorporated into a churchyard. Funeral processions would often take a specific route into church, according to the layout of yew trees. A yew sometimes overhung the lychgate, where a coffin would be laid to rest, and the priest and his clergymen would stand under another yew tree to greet the coffin-bearers.

YEW
Arils

The Fortingall Yew in Perthshire is believed to be at least 5,000 years old and has a surprising link in local folklore with the Roman governor Pontius Pilate. According to tradition, he was the son of a local woman and a Roman diplomat visiting a Pictish king, and he was either born under the tree or played in its branches. By the 1800s, the Fortingall Yew had developed a massive hollow trunk, creating an arch through which coffins were carried before a funeral.

One of Britain's three native conifers, the yew is dioecious, meaning that the trees are either male or female; recently, some interesting cases have arisen of old trees apparently changing sex. Cones on the male trees shed clouds of pollen in early spring, and from early September the female tree bears red, cup-like berries or 'arils', each containing a single seed. These are eaten by birds, such as thrushes and waxwings, which distribute the seeds via their droppings. The Irish yew, *Taxus baccata* var. *fastigiata*, grows in a denser, more compact form and is often planted in churchyards.

The yew's toxicity may have some surprising benefits: recent experiments have shown that chemical compounds called taxanes which are derived from the yew tree can be effective in treating cancer. While John Gerard, in the sixteenth century, was far from promoting any health benefits of the yew, he poured scorn on the old superstition that anyone who slept in its shade would die, saying that he and his school friends, when they were young, did so many times, and ate their fill of the berries.

With its dark green needles and bewilderingly dense canopy of branches, the yew casts a deep shade in which few wild flowers will grow. In his poem 'The Yew-tree on the Downs', D. H. Lawrence compares this to a secret sanctuary, and he draws the reader in:

> *... where the tent-cloths*
> *Curtain us in so dark*
> *That here we're safe from even the ermine moth's*
> *Twitching remark ...*
>
> THE COLLECTED POEMS OF D. H. LAWRENCE, VOLUME I, 1928

In 'Yew-Trees' (1803), inspired by a veteran tree in Lorton Vale, Cumbria, William Wordsworth celebrates the yew's contribution to the glory of former armies, and marvels at a living thing that seems to grow too slowly ever to decay. He wonders about the mysterious goings-on within the gloomy confines of an ancient yew:

> *... beneath whose sable roof*
> *Of boughs, as if for festal purpose, decked*
> *With unrejoicing berries, ghostly shapes*
> *May meet at noontide ...*

THE ANKERWYCKE YEW

RUNNYMEDE

When King John signed the famous Magna Carta or 'Great Charter', it is possible that he did so in the shade of the Ankerwycke Yew, which grows on an island close to the north bank of the River Thames. Historians speculate that the river in those days may have taken a more southerly course, so that Runnymede, the acknowledged site of the declaration, was on the same bank as Ankerwycke. Thought to be at least 2,000 years old, the yew tree was already ancient in the thirteenth century and may have been a site of pre-Christian worship. Runnymede is said to be the place where King Alfred held his *Witenagemot* or advisory council, and a Benedictine priory was established nearby in 1160.

Sealed on 15 June 1215, the Magna Carta was intended to pacify England's rebellious barons, promising swift justice and limits on feudal payments; in setting out the liberties of 'freemen' it is still regarded as one of the earliest charters recognising the rights of ordinary people. The Ankerwycke Yew may also have witnessed the courting of Anne Boleyn by King Henry VIII, and one story suggests that he proposed to her beneath its branches. Having lived through some key moments in English history, the Ankerwycke Yew is still thriving.

ACKNOWLEDGEMENTS

This book has been such a pleasure to write. I've always had a fascination for trees, but the discovery of so many lovely associations and traditions has been a wonderfully fulfilling experience.

My heartfelt love and thanks go to my husband, Colin, who has wandered through many woods with me, and I hope that we'll wander through many more. As an artist, he understands the personal input in creating something like this – he also reminds me to eat, when I'm lost in the writing! – and he gives me so much love and support. Likewise our two daughters, Verity and Leonie, are always so enthusiastic and excited about whatever I write, and listen patiently to my spoutings about history and customs.

I'd like to thank all the readers of my blog, The Hazel Tree, for your wonderful support and input over the eight or nine years that I've been writing it. I've made some fantastic friends and contacts all over the world, and exchanged vast quantities of information about all kinds of subjects – many of them tree-related. To find so many like-minded people, all sharing a deep appreciation for the natural world, is a very special thing. It proves to me that there are thousands of people out there who are quietly observing and caring about the environment, cherishing the stories, and understanding the value of a profound connection with nature.

My other thanks go to the writers, authors and naturalists whose works I have lovingly perused while researching this book. Whether their books are science-based, or collections of poetry or folklore, they have provided – and continue to provide – a hugely valuable resource that will inspire and inform generations to come. Friends and acquaintances have made suggestions about local customs to investigate, and I've also occasionally drawn on my own memory, from growing up in rural Shropshire.

I would like to thank Pavilion Books – in particular Peter Taylor, Nicola Newman and Gemma Doyle – for their enthusiasm and support, and at the National Trust I would like to thank Katie Bond, Amy Feldman, Emily Roe, Simon Toomer and Ray Hawes for casting their expert eyes over the text and making valuable suggestions. My grateful appreciation to Louise Morgan who has supplied the beautiful illustrations for this book, perfectly capturing the essential character and habit of each tree.

I'd also like to say that the whole experience of writing this has enhanced my own appreciation of trees – their beauty and variety in every season, and their immense value, not just to the environment but to ourselves, because we are an integral part of it. Looking back at old texts, it's easy to see that we knew our connection with nature in centuries gone by; we haven't lost it, but sometimes we just forget. Walking in woodland and gazing up at trees helps us to rediscover that knowledge.

Bain, Clifton, *The Ancient Pinewoods of Scotland* (Sandstone, 2013).

Bain, Clifton, *The Rainforests of Britain and Ireland* (Sandstone, 2015).

Bevan-Jones, Robert, *The Ancient Yew* (Windgather Press, 2015).

Burns, Robert, *The Complete Poems and Songs* (Waverley, 2011).

Clare, John, *Selected Poems* (Faber & Faber, 2004).

Culpeper, Nicholas, *The Complete Herbal* (1653).

Deakin, Roger, *Wildwood* (Hamish Hamilton, 2007).

Evelyn, John, *Sylva, or a Discourse of Forest-Trees and the Propagation of Timber in His Majesty's Dominions* (1664).

Folkard, Richard, *Plant Lore, Legends and Lyrics* (Sampson Low *et al*, 1884).

Gerard, John, *The Herball or Generall Historie of Plantes* (John Norton, 1597).

Gilpin, William, *Remarks on Forest Scenery* (Blamire, 1791).

Hardy, Thomas, *The Complete Poems* (Macmillan, 1976).

Hemery, Gabriel and Simblet, Sarah, *The New Sylva* (Bloomsbury, 2014).

Hight, Julian, *Britain's Tree Story* (National Trust, 2011).

Jefferies, Richard, *Field and Hedgerow* (Longmans, Green & Co, 1900).

Keats, John, *The Complete Poems* (Wordsworth Editions, 1994).

Knight, Richard Payne, *The Landscape* (W. Bulmer & Co, 1795).

Loudon, John Claudius, *Arboretum et Fruticetum Britannicum* (Bohn, 1854).

Lyte, Henry, *A Niewe Herball* (1578).

Mabey, Richard, *Flora Britannica* (Sinclair-Stevenson, 1996).

Miles, Archie, *The British Oak* (Constable, 2013).

Miles, Archie, *The Trees That Made Britain* (BBC Books, 2006).

Milner, Edward, *Trees of Britain and Ireland* (Natural History Museum, 2011).

Nuttall, Gertrude Clarke, *Trees and How They Grow* (Cassell, 1913).

Payne, Christiana, *Silent Witnesses: Trees in British Art* (Sansom & Co., 2017).

Penn, Robert, *Woods: A Celebration* (National Trust, 2017).

Rackham, Oliver, *Trees and Woodland in the British Landscape* (J. M. Dent, 1976).

Rackham, Oliver, *The History of the Countryside* (J. M. Dent, 1986).

Rodger, Donald, Stokes, Jon and Ogilvie, James, *Heritage Trees of Scotland* (Forestry Commission Scotland, 2006).

Skinner, Charles, *Myths and Legends of Flowers, Trees, Fruits and Plants* (J. B. Lippincott, 1911).

Step, Edward, *Wayside and Woodland Trees* (Frederick Warne & Co., 1904).

Strutt, J. G., *Sylva Britannica, or Portraits of Forest Trees* (Longman *et al*, 1830).

Sutherland, Patrick and Nicolson, Adam, *Wetland: Life in the Somerset Levels* (Penguin, 1986).

Taplin, Kim, *Tongues in Trees* (Green Books, 1989).

Thiselton-Dyer, Thomas, *The Folk-lore of Plants* (Chatto & Windus, 1889).

Vickery, Roy, *A Dictionary of Plant Lore* (Oxford University Press, 1995).

Watkins, Alfred, *The Old Straight Track* (Methuen, 1925).

White, Gilbert, *The Natural History of Selborne* (Benjamin White, 1789).

Wordsworth, William, *The Collected Poems* (Wordsworth Editions, 1994).

239